Pine Trees and the Sky

By the same author

The Quality of Mercy – The Lives of Sir James and Lady Cantlie

Why Devolution?

History and Practice of the Law of Mines and Minerals

The Sea our Heritage – British Maritime Interests Past and Present

Under the pen name Jean Rowan:

Rufus – the story of a New Forest Pony

The Writing on the Blackboard

Pine Trees and the Sky

Jean Cantlie Stewart

SCOTTISH CULTURAL PRESS
EDINBURGH

First published 1998 by
Scottish Cultural Press
Unit 14, Leith Walk Business Centre,
130 Leith Walk, Edinburgh EH6 5DT
Tel: 0131 555 5950 ♦ Fax: 0131 555 5018
e-mail: scp@sol.co.uk

British Library Cataloguing in Publication Data
A catalogue entry for this book is available from the British Library

ISBN: 1 898218 97 8

Printed and bound by
Redwood Books, Trowbridge, Wiltshire

Contents

The author and her son

Preface

This is the story of life in a remote Highland glen and of country people whose values and culture endure unchanging because they are rooted in nature, nurtured in kinsmanship and motivated by the need to survive, sometimes against the odds. Not long ago the towns were peopled by country folk, who had migrated thither over the last two centuries in search of employment, and their roots remained in the villages they had left, but in the last 50 years a change has slowly been taking place. The sentiment of some modern townsmen from overlarge conurbations has been introduced into the country, bringing with it a new scale of values which do not always equate to reality and often present country pursuits in a new and unfavourable light.

I hope that this book, which draws liberally on Scottish traditions and culture, will help to restore the balance and to present not only the human friendships that abound in remote areas and the help people there give to each other, but also the mutual understanding and respect that exists in the country between mankind and the animal kingdom.

Acknowledgements

Parts of this book have been previously published in periodicals, which include *The Countryman, The Gamekeeper and Countryside, Winter Sports* and *The Country Gentleman's Association Magazine.* I would like to thank them, and those who have encouraged me to write this book and given me help, particularly my cousins and other kind people up and down the glen for whose unfailing patience I will always be grateful. I must also thank those who have provided photographs, original paintings and maps, particularly Mr Peter Foster, who designed and painted the cover and one of the illustrations; Aberdeen University who allowed me to reproduce the maps; and the *Press and Journal* for their permission to use a photograph. My thanks also go to the librarians in Aberdeen University Library and Moray Public Library who have been interested, helpful and extremely knowledgeable.

All reasonable steps have been taken to trace copyright, seek permission to publish and express acknowledgement.

Pine Trees and the Sky: Evening

Then from the sad west turning wearily,
I saw the pines against the white north sky,
Very beautiful, and still, and bending over
Their sharp black heads against a quiet sky.
And there was peace in them; and I
Was happy, and forgot to play the lover,
And laughed, and did no longer wish to die;
Being glad of you, O pine-trees and the sky!

Rupert Brooke

To the people of Corgarff and Strathdon,
past and present, whose kindness and
courage inspired this story

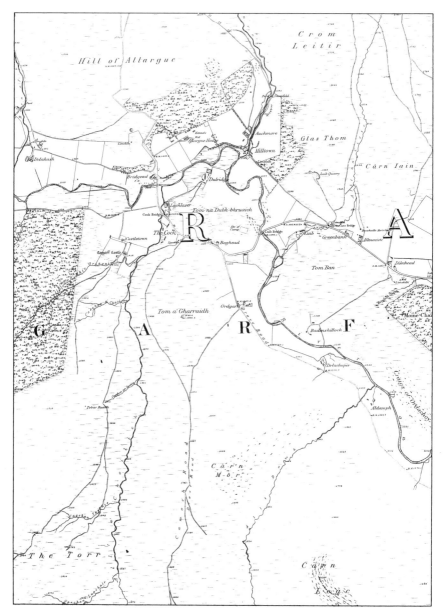

Map of the area surrounding Allargue, showing the Drove Road,
Corgarff Castle and the Hill of Allargue

1

In the High Hills

I first came to Corgarff in 1942, when my father took his only holiday in three years – and indeed his first full day off – from his job as Admiral Superintendent, Rosyth Royal Dockyard, and my brother and I were despatched as vanguards on bicycles, heading for the Highlands. We were overtaken by the family car just as the house of Allargue came into view after a train journey and then a 100 mile bicycle ride from Blairgowrie following the old military road north to Corgarff, Tomintoul and Fort George. Drowned rats were what we were by that time, for the heavens had opened upon us, turning the roads over the mountains into rivers through which we waded, pushing our bicycles up the formidable inclines, including the Devil's Elbow, and knocking on a door on the outskirts of Braemar to ask if we might eat our sandwiches in the porch, only to be invited in beside the fire. By the time we left the glens two weeks later, after an unforgettable holiday with our hospitable cousins, the octopus tentacles of this friendly and ancient civilisation had enveloped the whole family in their grasp. The wild remoteness and unchanging spiritual values of the natural world were the finest antidotes to the extremes of violence contorting mankind – of which we were spectators, swept up in the anxieties of the war at sea. Too young for national service I returned on a number of occasions in the next two years to help on hill and farm during vacations. Our association with the glen did not end in 1945, for my father managed the grousemoor for four successive summers in the late 1940s, while my cousin's husband was still a serving soldier. Thus it was natural that when a few years afterwards they were looking for a tenant for an empty house and I required, due to the crisis of divorce, a modest home for myself and my small son these two loose ends would tie together.

By this time Colonel Sir John Forbes had retired from the army and was farming the home farm. His family had owned lands in Strathdon for hundreds of years until his father – the fifth baronet – sold Castle Newe and the estate in 1922 and converted the old laundry into a comfortable home.

1

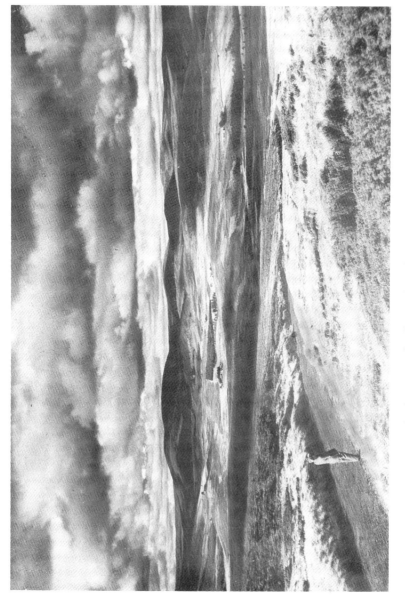

Looking towards Allargue from the Gairn Road

In 1933 John had married Agnes Wilson Farquharson, whose father, a Boer War hero, owned the lands of Allargue on the north side of the River Don at the head of the glen.

The cottage in which I was to make our home is veritably on the roof of the world. The path running in front of it is like the foredeck of a ship, from which the view is magnificent and uninterrupted. On the skyline opposite is a heather-clad mountain spur, capped by pines and larches and buttressed on its lower slopes by dykes and boulders. From this a stony field drops down steeply to a shallow valley and marshy bog, on the near side of which a steep bank leads up to the cottage. Through this burbles a mountain burn, small and friendly, except in flood, when it spreads – a greedy raging torrent – into the wide expanse below. On quiet summer days it never alters its note; despite its size it is full of tiny trout, and its rhythm provides the bass, as the cry of the wild birds supplies the treble, for the orchestra of natural sounds which pervade the silence of the hills. Circumventing the foundation stones of what was once a cluster of houses around a mill, to which the track passing the cottage leads down, the Milton burn then flows into the River Don, its deeper sounds muted for us by the distance and drop. On summer days the river's shallow water is transparent to its rocky bottom, but here and there at bends there are deep black pools from which froth eddies out over the larger stones. Because of its size and depth it is a dry fly river, except in spate, when it floods out over the whole valley, but using a worm upstream can, for less expert fishermen, be just as deadly. Half a mile downstream stands a two span stone bridge built on the Wade Adams design by the laird's great great grandfather and this provides a central focus for the view from the cottage and for the eye of the artist.

The glen is cut off from the rest of the world by two mountain ridges running east and west, one to the south and the other to the north, both of which continue on each side of the river for a number of miles before opening out into the lower strath. There are three roads leading in and out of the glen. The old military road, which comes over the mountains from the north was built after the 1745 Rebellion, when it went over the hill-tops and down into open country so that the Highlanders could not roll boulders on to troops in the narrow valleys below. In those days it followed a slightly different route, but now makes a precipitous descent to the river bridge, passing the Allargue Hotel and home farm at the bottom of the hill. After half a mile the old military road then short-cutted over two still extant Wade bridges to the foothills of the southern ridge, while the present road, developed from an old cattle route, continues eastward along the river to

Strathdon, passing the sub post office, the school and the church. An old toll house, where dues were collected – some roads were built and maintained by the lairds and some by public finance – stands at the road junction, where the way south now leads off from the main road over the hills to re-join the old military route half way up the ascent. The village of Corgarff is the last clachan of houses on the river and the house of Allargue sits in a high exposed position, perched like an eagle's nest on the northern slopes below the trees, which divide farmland from the mountains behind. Only a track suitable for ponies follows the river westward to its source in the wild heartland of the Cairngorms, although there is also a deep V, which it is said a giant cut into the tip of the southern ridge for the benefit of intrepid foot travellers. Below it stands a pine wood from which a sandy track leads down to an ancient tower house within a high protective wall. Corgarff Castle, built around 1550 and used as a fortified hunting lodge, was fired by the Jacobites in 1689, remaining dilapidated until garrisoned by government troops after the 1745, who were not withdrawn until 1831. The Castle is ideally placed to keep an eye on all the routes leading into the glen.

When we first came to the cottage smoke rose from the chimneys of the eight houses which can be seen from the front door. By the time we left in 1973 only three were occupied except by visitors at holiday time – such has been the drift away from the glens during those years. To the west beyond the hotel and almost out of view lie a number of farms flanking the north river bank for three miles and reached only by a stony track. The most remote fell into disrepair decades ago and the others are now used as holiday cottages. A hundred years ago a road ran along the bottom of our garden, linking the mill below us with the old military way over the hill and a canal – now dry – edged with stones led an arm of water from the burn to work the mill thresher, with a grassed circular well in which, when the water was low, a horse walked round at an even pace to keep the mill wheel turning. Then the glens rang with voices and even sixty years ago there were still forty children in the school, whereas there were less than twenty in our time. 'Here is the mill,' wrote Robert Louis Stevenson, in his poem 'Keepsake Mill', 'with the humming of thunder. Here is the weir with the wonder of foam. Here is the sluice with the race running under'. Although his next verse begins, 'Sounds of the village grow stiller and stiller', this is only because his imaginary children leave and return in old age, whereas now all around us the silence is profound, broken only by the bleating of sheep and the cries of birds. The inhabitants have gone, taking with them one of the most ancient civilisations in our island. Although many of the

The upper reaches of the Don looking towards Ben Avon
(from a watercolour by Peter Foster)

old ways persist and the old manners are maintained, nevertheless, when the pibroch sounds in the glen on Armistice Day, it is as much a lament for the dead of earlier wars and for those who emigrated to the four corners of the earth, as it is for those who died defending democracy in the two World Wars. Great work have they all done but behind them the glens have been emptied of people, as 'One by one the voices faded and the hills slept'.

Behind the house the field rises steeply to a high hill – the back of the cottage deeply embedded in the rocky soil. In a good summer, all along the grassy track which leads – level with the roof – past the back of the house and away through the remains of a larch wood to the heather beyond, the springy mountain turf is alive with the colour of wild flowers which grow in profusion. Within a quarter of a square mile there are nearly fifty different species, whose names the local people never need to verify in books. These include pink and white clover, thyme, pansy (violet, blue and cream), vetch, tufted vetch, buttercup, rock rose, common tormentil, coltsfoot, speedwell, birds foot trefoil, vipers bugloss, dog daisy, bluebell (the English harebell), star of Bethlehem, forget-me-not, stitchwort, ladies mantle, tanzy, dead nettle, sorrell, thistle, common yarrow, ribwort, plaintain, common eyebright, vervain, pig nut, milkwort (white and blue), fumitory, common ragwort, ragged robin, yellow bedstraw, daisy, stonecrop and dandelion. A quarter of a mile further on, following and climbing up from the burn, the springy turf gives way to heather. Beyond lie the mountains, the corries, the peat bogs and the burns, which are the dwelling place of the grouse, the black cock, the grey hen, the capercaillie, the mountain hare and the red deer, which graze in competition with the black faced mountain sheep. When we lived in the cottage the buzzards and hawks were considered to be dangerous predators, but now all birds of prey are protected and the effect on the grouse and other smaller birds has been disastrous. Just before we left four plantations of fir trees were planted among the heather which have become the breeding grounds for these birds of prey.

Summers are short for both flora and fauna, for even in late spring the snow lies on in the deeper corries and bogs and in June glimpses of the white Cairngorm peaks can still be seen from the top of the hill. Then after the snow melts the mountain sides are alive with the colours of summer, as the sun sweeps in ever changing patterns of light across the heather, which in August and September bursts into dramatic purple. In the evening just as dusk is beginning to fall this light strikes with such suddenness and inten-sity that the greens, purples and browns on one hillside are momentarily illuminated as if with the strength of a searchlight. Then just as swiftly the daylight dies and dusk drops on what only seconds before was a scene of pure magic. In these high hills nature provides a canvas so dramatic that many of the desires of the heart and of the senses can be satisfied without recourse to the purse. Here a person feels that he owns everything in nature while owning nothing in material wealth. Sometimes, after a storm, the arc of a rainbow spans the hills, splashed across the sky with a suddenness that no human painter could ever match. For a moment both ends of the rainbow are so close and so real that it seems one could run and touch them and that one is actually standing beneath the arch of pink, gold, blue and turquoise. Then, more inconstant even than the sunlight, the rainbow fades and flames out again on another hillside, the rich variations of colours blending together in the distance, like paint upon the palate of an artist.

There is a fable that this moorland estate on the south facing bank of the river, encompassing rounded mountains, burns, open valleys and stony farmland was granted to my cousin's family by the Earl of Mar when, on a hunting expedition, he became lost in a fierce blizzard and was given such generous and life-saving hospitality by Robert Farquharson, one of his tenants, that he gifted all the land that could be seen up and down the river on the north side to him and his heirs in perpetuity. Whether or not there is truth in this whimsical story, the land certainly came by gift from the Earl of Mar in 1645 to the family who have owned it for three and a half centuries. Only the big house and the dower cottage date in their construction from the original grant and, although the big house was twice enlarged, hidden in the interior can still be seen the eye and hand of the original architect, whose design remains untouched in the dower cottage. Many castles and houses in Scotland built during these times of conflict put security before the importance of graceful lines. There are plentiful examples of fortified hunting lodges, manor houses and steadings both in these glens and further north, securely fenced around by walls and farm buildings, or with only arrow slit windows to protect them from marauders. Yet here were two houses of modest size, planned with proportions satisfying to the eye, whose only defence against marauders and the weather was the almost total lack of windows in the north wall, and the stout bar hidden in the cavity of the wall which protected the entrance from intruders. This was the period of Cromwell's Protectorate, with the whole of the violent history of the Covenanting period and of the '15 and '45 Rebellions still to come. Although there were many incidents of burning, murder and rape in Scotland before and at this time (indeed in 1571

Corgarff Castle was put to the torch by Adam Gordon of Auchindoun, who massacred in this way Margaret Forbes, her children and servants) nevertheless this unhappy suffering did not perpetuate itself in this glen. Instead, following the tradition of the local fable explaining the original grant of land, these two houses and those of the surrounding tenants, then made of rough stone and probably heather thatched and now ruined or replaced, offered hospitality and happiness to all who came.

When I began to renovate the cottage it had reached that state of disrepair which marks the no man's land between ruin and reclamation. Unless aid came soon the interior would be lost. In the first stage of neglect the interior can be saved almost in its entirety; in the second it must be stripped out; in the third, wood rot inside and the weather outside and possibly dry rot in the stone have all acted together to affect the whole structure. In this instance the structure and the roof were sound, although rising damp had seriously affected the plaster and woodwork on the ground floor to a height of between one or two feet. Ivy was growing in below the sitting room windows. The walls were rough harled and in some places peeling and they had been painted dirty white with the residue from the gas carbide plant at the big house. The chimney pots were either missing or leaning at crazy angles and also leaning was a do-it-yourself corrugated iron porch stuck like a red nose on the face of the house. In the seventeenth century the walls had been built in an unusual way, for a line of huge irregularly shaped rocks had been rolled together to provide a foundation which stretched upwards eighteen inches from the ground. The only square dressed stones were the two on either side of the front door. Like the early Christian Church the house was literally built upon a rock. The same principles of construction had originally been used in the big house, except that the rooms were larger. Even now these proportions create the same satisfaction to the viewer, lines are not straight by the surveyor's ruler but straight by the eye, which allows for the perspective of distance. Allargue was twice enlarged. The old part of the house eventually became the north elevation. Wings were added, one of which was later incorporated into a new facade facing south.

Behind one of the double doors of the cottage is a stout square-sided wooden bar which slides into the cavity of the wall, of similar design to that used by Katherine Bar-the-Door who tried to save the life of James I by putting her arm through the brackets to hold back his pursuers, while he was being lowered into a hiding place beneath the floor. Here, however, there are no brackets. Instead, the bar is so long and the cavity so deep that it slides out to the middle of the double doors while still leaving sufficient length within the wall to provide an unbreakable bolt. On the left hand side of the small rectangular hall is a sitting room, on the other a dining room, with a one storey kitchen beyond, a more recent addition to the house. A passage leads away from the hall to a curving stair which is lit by the only window in the back wall of the house, at the top of which a landing leads to three bedrooms. The panelled doors and upstairs floors are untouched by woodworm, because they were cut from the ancient forests of old Scots fir, renowned for the hardness of its wood, which is never grown now because of the length of time it takes to mature. Once upon a time the floors downstairs would have been flagged, but now these splendid stones form the path along the front of the house and cement has been laid in their place except in the sitting room, where a more recent wooden floor is fixed to rafters resting upon the earth.

One of those who enjoyed the sanctuary of the dower cottage in the late eighteenth century was Janet, the laird's daughter, who had two illegitimate children by the eldest son of the Andersons of Candacraig, who had owned land in Strathdon since the twelfth century. Not wanting to marry her he defended a case which she brought against him in the Court of Session to force his hand in matrimony, replying that he did not wish to marry the daughter of a man 'who was nothing but a pedlar'. She won her case, and, despite the acrimony upon which their marriage was founded, they enjoyed a happy and prolific wedlock. Later, the cottage became the home farm, where thirteen children were reared in the living memory of the youngest daughter, who explained that they would not all have been home at one time. Then, after the addition of a kitchen and provision of a bathroom under the stairs, it became the retirement home for the cook from the big house, who took the laird's relations as paying guests. When she died it was let as a holiday home to the daughter of the previous much loved local doctor, who owned one of the first motor cars in the glen; then to a retired couple who made their pennies stretch by parsimonious living and then, after a period empty except for occasional holidays, to ourselves on a 'friendly' improvement and repairing agreement. The atmosphere of the cottage is one of security and peace, the only enemies being those of which the nursery rhyme warns, 'The north wind doth blow and we shall have snow'. As soon as I began work renovating the house I heard this wind moaning against the north wall. Nevertheless it seemed that louder than the noise of any wind the house was saying to me as clearly as if it had been a voice at my shoulder, 'Don't worry. You are safe here'.

2

'The Auld Hoose'

Fearing the neglect awaiting me in the cottage, for the first few days after my arrival in the glen I did not dare peep inside but dug in the garden, overgrown with weeds. As soon as the tradesmen arrived, however, their kindness and enthusiasm gave the venture a friendly, hopeful light and this acted as a spur to my will. Mr Comfort the plumber came first, resplendent in sombre black suit and bowler hat, having attended a funeral. He was an outstanding local dignitary, who insisted on high standards both for himself and for his sons and employees. He had a pungent wit and no illusions about humanity, 'There's naethin' in some folks,' he warned his sons, 'but what the spoon puts in.' Entering the cottage together we gazed in astonishment at the large black sooty hole which served as fireplace in the dining room, the cooking stove having been moved into the kitchen by a former tenant. On one side of this stood an upright iron 'sway', which supported an ancient iron kettle from a hook fixed to its hinged arm. Mr Comfort did not approve of my idea of providing hot water by means of a coal fire, which would heat the dining room day and night. Although I won the argument, the presence of guests, whom he saw in his mind's eye as increasing in number with equivalent demands for hot water, eventually compelled us to add a calor gas booster in the kitchen, where, unhampered by demarcation problems, his son built a huge drying cupboard round the hot tank to house the wet clothes endemic to the Highlands. Before the plumber's new brick fireplace was finished the laird's sisters presented the cottage with an imposing yellow pine mantelpiece which came out of Castle Newe (demolished in 1927), having spent half a century stored in their garage. It gave an air of graceful antiquity to the room.

With this accomplished, the plumber persuaded me to bring all pipes under one roof in order to avoid frost. When the bath and handbasin had been fitted into the little room under the stairs, which was lit from a frosted window into the hall, a back door had been made on the stairs opening into a wooden shed leading both outside and to a lavatory. 'Put the lavatory into the bathroom,' the plumber said. 'The house will never be comfortable till you do and it won't freeze,' adding, when I demurred about cost, 'I'm nae verra punctual about sending my bills.' Although his other accounts arrived in the normal way the one for moving the lavatory did not materialise for three years to the day. I was grateful for his kind concern – it was typical of the way that hill folk look after each other – and when pennies and guests multiplied the wooden erection at the back of the house was replaced by harled cement blocks and turned into storage space and a tiny bedroom.

Next to arrive were the masons, a father and two sons by the name of Smith from over the hill, small and wiry and full of ideas about what to do to renovate the cottage at minimum cost. They ran up ladders, straightened chimney cans, added more, patched up the peeling harling on the walls and replaced cracked windows (cheerfully and apologetically breaking others as they did so). They worked extraordinarily fast and their estimates were unbelievably low, but to balance this their hours of work were chaotic and since they were not on the telephone I had no control at all over their movements. No doubt impressed by my new dungarees, they imagined my professional knowledge was greater than it was but when they saw the reverse was the truth they were generous with tips about how to do the work. When renewing the rotten downstairs skirting boards, they inevitably left large gaps of up to a foot above where the lathe and plaster was rotten. As fast as I put plaster into the holes it dropped down inside the new skirtings. 'Fill the holes with newspaper and plaster on that,' said the masons as they drank their 'fly' cups of tea, 'and posterity will know by the date of the newspaper when the work was done.' This information enabled me to plaster with greater confidence and under their instruction I discovered the exact moment to polish when the plaster was drying. I was now able to pull out the ivy growing in below the windows and to restore the walls to their former smoothness.

While the sons worked outside their father built a new fireplace in the sitting room, where the feet of the mantelpiece were crumbling with wet rot and the fireplace tiles were broken and missing. Again we had a gaping hole, this time framed by stone uprights and lintel. After the masons had left in the evening I saw that one upright was loose and that there was granite behind. Intrigued, I fetched a crowbar from the shed and pulled the upright a little further from the wall which made my heart somersault. My impatience taught me a lesson – it is safer to leave skilled and heavy jobs to a man. Not only are they physically stronger, but they understand by instinct and training the right way to approach a task. The experiment, however, was a success. We found next day a granite surround hidden inside the first, flush with the wall, which, with wire wool, could be polished to an attractive grey. Providing the mason with a drawing of a friend's fireplace, with two little nooks on either side, I watched him copy it meticulously for the small sum of £5 and since no kind friend came forward with another mantelpiece I fitted instead a wooden beading between the granite and the wall. Appreciating this finish, a representative of the Historic Buildings Council later told me that fireplaces were originally installed flush with the wall and that it is only within the last two or three hundred years that they have been made to stand out into the room to make them more imposing.

One of the masons' tasks was to block up the frosted window into the hall and make a new bathroom window to the north. Once it was installed I realised why no one had put it in before. Since the snow piled up against that wall the bathroom had developed a form of dry rot without spores, apparently common only to coal mines. Any wood or plaster near the window crumbled and by the following year the only solution was to plaster the sides and sill of the window embrasure with pure cement. Soon, however, it became apparent that this was part of a wider problem, for no plaster on any part of the north wall of the bathroom lasted for more than months. I therefore strapped it with wood, leaving a six inch air space and so impressed was the local joiner with my work that he invited me down to see his workshop. But again I learnt the lesson that if you trespass into men's work you must be 'canny'. At a crucial moment my screw driver slipped and removed a piece of skin from my nose, just missing my eye. Joinery may resemble dressmaking, but the tools are more dangerous and require more strength to control than scissors and pins.

Jimmy, the younger son of Mr Shand, the grocer in Strathdon – whose elder son Sandy ran a splendid travelling van from the shop – gave me my first lessons in joinery. He was working away from home but, returning at weekends and hearing I required help, he arrived, a debonair young man with a hammer at his waist, to see what he could do in answer to a minor crisis. Removing and breaking up for firewood the worm eaten 'slab' door between the dining and kitchen rooms, I had set out in a landrover with Zilla, Agnes' eldest daughter, to bring home a panelled door from one of the derelict farm houses far out to the west. It looked easy and we had taken a vast array of tools, but the screws had been there for hundreds of years and only determination allowed us to succeed. Triumphant we returned only to find that, since we had no measurements, the door was too broad and short. Undismayed, I started to saw just as Bob, my cousin's gardener and handyman, who farmed the croft opposite, came in with a message. 'You're daein' that all wrang,' he commented, 'leave it the noo and I'll come back after my tea.' Bob had a reputation for avoiding heavy work, but his chivalry was greater than any reputed idleness and all I had to do was to start a job to encourage him to come immediately to my rescue – a duodenal ulcer had no doubt contributed to his caution. Once the door was hung we had a large gap at the top. This was the moment of Jimmy's entry and soon we had a shelf with glass above it on which I put a line of china horses to remind me of the real horses of my youth. Then Jimmy took the doors off the cupboard on the north wall of the sitting room and carried them upstairs to make a fitted wardrobe. He warned me that the bottom of the sitting room cupboard was too damp ever to dry out and so he made a dummy cupboard to block off the lower part. Then, while he sawed and planed bookshelves, I lined the upper back wall of the now open cupboard under his tuition, and finally he cut a plywood arch for the top, following the points of compass circles, which we drew to get a pleasing curve.

By the time work started on the kitchen Jimmy was working further from home, but my cousin recommended the two Morgan brothers who were in partnership in Strathdon and, when I telephoned to say I had found toadstools growing in profusion in the kitchen walk-in cupboards, they arrived in their van in the first snowstorm of the winter to see what they could do to help. 'Will you get back?' I asked as we sailed down blithely over the rough track. 'Aye, we'll easily manage,' came the reply. Their antidote to the toadstools was asbestos. 'Nae, it's nae dry rot,' they assured me, 'just the sort of fungus you'd find outside.' Sure enough their asbestos sheets stood the test of time, did not give us any fell disease and allowed us to forget that underneath the shelves there was an unwelcome invasion. While they painted the dining room ceiling I started work under their watchful eye on chipping off with a chisel and hammer all the tens of layers of paint on the walls. Soon Bob came to my rescue in the evenings to finish this job and now all that remained inside was for me to strip off the old wall paper, scrape and wax the fir doors back to their original colour, and paint the skirtings and walls.

Outside also the work was progressing. Concerned about the safety of the rickety old farm shed, built of wood and corrugated iron, my cousin asked Bob to demolish it and when I asked him to do the same for the equally dangerous and unsightly corrugated iron porch the whole shaky erection collapsed almost at the first blow of the sledge hammer. Never

Auchmore during renovations (the porch has already been demolished)

regretting its departure, I nevertheless was immediately aware that now when the wind was strong it whistled under the front doors with such force that you were not sure whether you were inside in the house or outside in the gale. Why, when I passed through the hall when the wind was blowing, did I always find the words of John Keats coming into my mind, 'Old Meg she was a gypsy and dwelt upon the moor'? After we were installed in the cottage we hung thick dyed blankets as curtains to stop the draught and put 'snakes' filled with sand along the bottoms of the double doors, but all were useless. Then, spotting later in a Georgian house similar double front doors which, opening within the confines of the outside wall allowed space for a pair of internal doors also opening inwards, we copied the idea and, although our four feet walls did not give quite sufficient clearance we were able to hang the internal doors an inch or two into the hallway. The results were dramatic. At last the elements were kept at bay.

Life was now starting to be a race against time. I knew I was welcome with my cousins until Christmas, when all five daughters would be home, but by that date the cottage must be ready for habitation. In the depth of winter I proposed to leave it under the snow and stay with parents, relatives and friends until the spring. Unfortunately the light began to go in the afternoon just as the first snow of the winter arrived and this coincided with the delivery of a parcel of special paint for the sitting room. On the first day of the storm the snow was very deep, but I knew that if I did not go down to the cottage I would be seen as a 'softie from the south'. So, wading in drifts to my thighs, I threw the parcel of paint ahead of me and picked it up again, and when I reached the cottage boiled up snow in a kettle on a paraffin stove to water down the paint, for by this time we had turned off the water in the cottage. All this time, since the very early days of the renovation, my small son had been staying up at the big house under the watchful eye of my cousin's Nanny, who had returned to do the cooking now that all five fledglings were flown. Her decision had followed a few months in the bright lights of London, but she had returned, preferring the social life of Corgarff. She had a beautiful singing voice and used to sing duets in the war with one of the local farmers to my cousin's accompaniment on the piano. Her happy optimism conveyed itself to everyone and her favourite sayings were, 'Oh we'll easily manage' and 'Someone will do it'. One afternoon I came back to find her dancing round the kitchen with Hugh in her arms, singing the accompaniment and the words of a Scottish waltz, the expression on his face one of joy and self-consciousness.

I realised that unless I could find a form of lighting more efficient than paraffin lamps and thus extend the shortened afternoons, I was going to lose the race against the clock. Agnes therefore accompanied me to the attic to find an Aladdin lamp, put away when the carbide gas plant was installed in the big house. Acetylene gas generated by carbide was once a popular form of lighting in houses without electricity. It gave a beautiful soft light and was made by mixing carbide and water in a gas house. Huge drums of carbide powder had to be opened with an axe and the residue dumped after the gas had been extracted. One day a safety inspector arrived without warning to see what was going on and was alarmed at the degree of hazard which accompanied the operation. Just at the psychological moment, therefore, when he was starting to raise objections, the gardener volunteered the remark, 'And do you know when the weather is cold, I aye puts in a lighted stove'. This added horror had the desired effect. Out of his depth and realising that at this height and remoteness no regulations could be enforced, the inspector beat a hasty retreat. We found the Aladdin lamp, which, although running on paraffin, had a mantle instead of a wick, so that it could be pumped up to produce a stronger light. Now, with improved lighting, I extended my afternoon work and achieved my target. Two years later we installed calor gas lighting downstairs (by which form of energy we already cooked) and a decade after that, in company with my cousins, I put in a second-hand electric generator.

By Christmas the cottage was ready for occupation, but outside there were still repairs and improvements which awaited our return in the spring, with tractors and trailers ferrying furniture between van and cottage. First, I wanted a garage for my car, but where could I put it? Suddenly I had the answer. If I removed the flowers in front of the cottage I would just be able to drive the car along the path above the rockery, at the end of which there was space for a lean-to extension to the coal shed. My eye alighted on the old corrugated iron sheets and beams that still lay in a heap and I asked George Morrison, the near-by farmer if he could perhaps give me a hand. It was a dream of make believe, made more so by George bringing with him a friend who was 'fu'. Suddenly by mistake, one of the beams dropped upon me – a fitting end to a daft do-it-yourself scheme that I should never have attempted. In the hotel next day I interrupted George telling the story with all good humour. Nevertheless, determined not to be beaten, I asked the Morgan brother to return and, using the corrugated iron sheets and four small tree trunks they gave me the shed I wanted. Now I could get my car into the garage, but could only get out and along the front of the house in reverse. I needed a turning space, but by then it was August and everyone was on the hill. This time Bob's son, Roger, a boy of twelve, came to my rescue and together we barrowed the beams from the demolished shed, boulders, rubbish and earth to build a projection out on to the slope beneath. Nervously, knowing what lay beneath, I drove on to it. It held, but then I found we had buried the outside water tap, which I would have to do without until I could afford to install another. However, so successful did we feel the project had been that Roger returned to use the grooved lining of the old porch to box in the bath and keep the woodlice away from our feet.

The second addition to the cottage outbuildings – the stable – was built seven years later. When I bought Hugh's first pony we made a tiny loose box in the coal shed, but there was no room for the second pony, so back came the masons and built an extension wall to the coal shed, flush with the front of the house, leaving just sufficient space for two small pony boxes and a coal bunker. Finally, when the electric generator arrived we put doors on the garage and housed the engine beside the car. The provision of even such low wattage electricity was indeed a turning point in our lives. Just months before we moved away a maiden speech by the new Member of Parliament highlighted the needs of the glen and not long afterwards the Hydro Electric arrived, developed out of a hydro scheme started by the Wallaces of Candacraig for the people of Strathdon. The benefits of civilisation were at hand, the old ways of the glen were dying and new ways were being born.

Auchmore after renovation

3

The Glory of the Garden

To create a garden is always an enjoyable challenge, but to create one at 1,400 feet, even if only of pocket size, is a task that brings many setbacks. 'Such gardens are not made', wrote Rudyard Kipling, 'By saying, "Oh how beautiful" and sitting in the shade, While better men than we go out and start their working lives, By grabbing weeds from gravel paths with broken dinner knives'. Broken knives we had in profusion after my exertions in the cottage, but also plants bravely surviving from a bygone age, such as honeysuckle, gentians, autumn crocuses, japonica, wild primroses and, surprisingly, even a single fuschia hidden from the frost among the weeds and fruit bushes. Southern gardens have level lawns on which to play ball games of every kind, Highland cottage gardens are all on a slope; they have flowers in front of the house, fruit bushes at the bottom of the garden and vegetables and potatoes in between. Even eight miles down the glen, often protected by fences and stone walls from winds and marauding animals, gardens grow in profusion, but as the river winds on towards its source the season becomes so short that it threatens to be over before the flowers and vegetables have blossomed and ripened, unless they are lying in a south facing garden which catches the sun.

We soon found that a frost in June can be sufficiently sharp to ruin the whole strawberry crop and when winter comes the snow is so heavy that it breaks branches and shrubs with indiscriminate ruthlessness. Because of our remoteness from human habitation we were also pestered by marauding animals which could destroy in a few minutes the work of years. Bad winters bringing the snow to the height of fences provided inviting thoroughfares leading straight from the hill to the young bark of a favourite tree or flowering shrub, which, if drifting laid it bare, would be stripped almost to the ground. To prevent this winter invasion of red and roe deer, mountain hares and rabbits our predecessors had built a high entanglement of wire netting, supported by an extraordinary assortment of twigs and branches, which was now so dilapidated that it gave no protection whatsoever, even from the cows and sheep, which grazed the open pasture around the cottage. The favourite time for the cross-Highland cows to arrive in the garden was five in the morning. We were woken with a start from a deep sleep by the sound of thumps and coughing and blowing through the nostrils and the next minute in our night clothes all of us, my son Hugh (now two years old), my kind student help and any guests staying would be running through the garden making ferocious noises to scare off these ungainly visitors, who gazed at us in astonishment under horned and furrowed brows.

The first task was to demolish this now useless fence and get help from John Reid, the postie, who was also a fencer and a farmer, to put up a new one. Surprisingly when I asked at Shand's shop where I could get the posts I was told, 'You get them here', and down they went on our usual weekly order, sandwiched between sugar and biscuits. Curiously enough, eighteenth-century General Wade, the bridge builder, had also listed his accounts in the same way, for the cost of the carriage of biscuits is followed by that for his building stones. With the posts securely driven in we put up the wire and netting ourselves in order to save money. Then, determined to have a level lawn, despite our slope, on which to play games, we started digging and moving soil on sacks. Hugh thought this was a splendid game, and, clutching the Labrador puppy, rode a-top the pile, cheerfully adding to its weight. The removal of the soil meant that we now had to build a second rockery below that supporting the foundations of the cottage and a herbaceous border with a wall beyond to hold back the new lawn. There was no shortage of plants from the gardens of kind friends or of fallen dykes from which the stones could come but all had to be barrowed or carried. Below this wall we sowed vegetables and added raspberries and gooseberries to the black and red currant bushes, which looked as though they had been in the cottage garden since the start of time.

By the following summer it became apparent that the rabbits and black faced mountain sheep did not think much of us as fencers. The latter either jumped our fence or knocked it down and the rabbits burrowed underneath or worked away at a weak part of the fence until they had a tiny hole. My parents could not bear to see my disappointment and kindly said they would pay any necessary account. Back came John Reid, the postie/fencer, with new wire and rabbit netting and peace now temporarily reigned. It was not so, however, at the 'big house', where my cousins also had been saving on fencing bills. Once upon a time there had been an internal fence for the flower garden, just as there still was for the vegetables, but this had been removed, because, with secure field fencing, no sheep had been seen for years in the policies. Unfortunately word got round among the sheep population that there were good pickings to be had in the neighbourhood of the house, and, as in the old Scottish proverb that, 'He who sups sleeps', on one particularly cold night two sheep (one at least of which must have been a pet lamb) arrived in the kitchen to keep warm. Startled by humans entering they moved on to the front hall and then down a passage to the smoking room before being finally shooed out of the front door. The weather continuing wintry, the following day they returned, and, when they were again going to be shown the door, one of them made a dash for the stairs, and into the front bedroom, calling in at the bathroom on the way. Disturbed, the miscreant considered a wild leap through the window, but thinking better of it dashed back down the stairs and out through the dining room window shattering the glass. An amused and artistic friend encapsulated this story in an etching which hangs now by the smoking room fire. Two sheep sit cross legged in arm chairs, one smoking a pipe, the other knitting and one is saying to the other, 'We have a very nice kitchen, bedroom and bathroom too'.

'Very nice kitchen, bedroom, and bathroom too!' by Hubert Leschallas

Our own reprieve was only temporary for, although we now had the larger animals at bay, we were soon to be troubled by those most pertinacious and troublesome of all creatures – rats. For the first year we had seen no sign of them, but this was because they were attracted by the warmth and feed in the steading of the farm just below the cottage. Then the farmer, while still farming the land, moved house and shifted the contents of his steading five miles down the glen. He still continued to put out poison, but the rats began to seek shelter on their journey to and from the river in our buildings rather than his. We were told by the experts that this had, in fact, been one of their routes for a long time. Although I learnt to admire the courage and cunning of these little animals, I never learnt to like them. The first sign that something was wrong was when holes began to appear in the rockery. At first we thought it was moles, for they led to deep underground passages which caused boulders to subside and kill valuable plants. Then the vegetables and strawberries started to disappear and we became increasingly disquieted. One evening I heard stealthy noises by the front door which worked up into a crescendo of bangs and crashes, as the rats, having come through the old loose mortar between the foundation stones, proceeded to make a thoroughfare amongst the rubble behind the lathe and plaster. Eventually this route led, most unfortunately, to the skirting board behind the head of my bed and this now seemed to form the spearhead of their advance. Rats are very punctual creatures; they work to a demanding time-table, by which it is possible to set the clocks. They entered the outside walls at 7 p.m., went out again about an hour and a half later and returned exactly at 10, 'Just as the pubs shut', said Howie Kellas, one of the Strathdon posties, with typical wit. Having put in some active gnawing and dismantling work behind my bed they then settled down to sleep in the wee sma' hours, followed by races and exercises up above our heads just before light. With the first streaks of dawn back they went to the great outside. A busy programme for them and no sleep for us.

By this time Bob had moved to a more responsible job and a milder climate further south and Mr Webster, the new gardener/handyman at the big house – who was known for some reason as 'Ole Man River' – came down to advise me. We must, he said, discover their runs and we could do this by looking for areas of disturbed earth under wood piles and in sheds and for the brushing marks that their fur makes trailing through grass or loose soil. Here we must put down oatmeal poison. The trouble was that there were too many rats for this to make much difference. With one gone another came and the sleepless nights continued. He also advised not to block the holes until we had got rid of the infestation, because I might easily shut a rat inadvertently into the house which might then gnaw his way out at night into the bedroom. At last, in desperation, I was driven to set gin traps, now illegal. It is indeed a cruel method of extermination, but as the death roll mounted quickly to a dozen and a half and there were fewer and fewer entries for the midnight steeplechase I was not over-troubled by conscience and instead, against professional advice, baited the traps with oatmeal poison. At last we felt the moment had come to block the holes between the rocks at the front of the house. The silence continued, but we congratulated ourselves too soon. Their little paws tore out the mortar and we had to remix the cement with broken glass. This time the silence would have been maintained had we not entered upon a further programme of soil shifting.

The house was suffering from rising damp and we were advised that if we removed the earth from the back of the cottage this would help to make it dry. It was a little time before I was sufficiently brave to proceed, because for one thing we did not know whether the cottage had originally been built into the bank with insufficient foundations or whether the soil had slowly built up behind it to a height of about three feet. Fortunately it was the latter and all we needed was a bulldozer. Nevertheless it would be a tricky job. We decided we would put the spare soil outside the front gate to make a parking space for cars and a bank for daffodils. I telephoned a local contractor who promised to come in good time. One evening I returned home to find a bulldozer parked by the gate and mounds of earth deposited at the far end of the house in huge castles. It looked as if a giant had been digging sand castles on a beach. The lad who arrived next morning to drive the machine had only just left school. Had he been one year older I would have taught him while teaching for a spell at the local junior secondary school. It was a pity I had not taught him because we had a failure of communication. He was a splendid operator and the earth disappeared as if by magic and reappeared in the wrong place. When I asked him to do something different, he replied, 'It winna dae that'. To him the machine had a will of its own and he dusted the cab before leaving as though it was a dinky toy. When he skirted so close to the building that the back wall of the coal shed developed a crack I knew I had had enough. I telephoned his father who said he would come next day. He arrived, gave his son instructions and left. Now when his son said 'It winna dae that', I replied, 'Your father says it must be done that way'. Knowing his father was behind me he persuaded the machine to do what I wanted provided I could be heard above the roar of its engine. Soon the earth was all deposited and levelled in front of the gate. After he had gone I began rolling it in with the wheels of my car. Unfortunately there was a large pointed stone in the middle of it and suddenly to my horror there I was stuck on top of it unable to move. Not only did I have to summon help from Massie's garage eight miles away, but when the men came (Jimmy Thomson wisely did not come alone) they had to lift the car clear of the rock.

Now that the earth was removed it was necessary to hold back the bank with rocks and grass and then to lay a drain along the back of the house taking surface water away to the burn. Robbie, on whose farm the gravel quarry was located, came to help, arriving with a trailer full of huge stones to support the bank and track. Under them we placed a line of turfs and soil which I sowed with grass, temporarily covering everything with wire netting. By the time the plumber arrived to dig the drain I was worrying about the fall, so I asked my cousin John to come down and check. But he was more interested in the nest of a yellow hammer which he found in the wire netting at the bottom of the bank. The nest was duly moved and then put back and the yellow hammer returned, but after everyone had gone it began to pour with rain and I waited in vain for the water to emerge. Weeks went by and nothing happened. Could the plumber have got his measurements wrong? The mason was coming up the road to fix a missing slate so cautiously I asked him if he could bring his measuring equipment. When he arrived he told me with a twinkle that he had met the plumber but that the equipment had been covered with his coat. Sure enough the fall was sufficient. That very night it rained again and water poured from the pipe. I knew it had to be right, for the plumber's excellent reputation went far and wide. 'When I go through the country,' he once said to me, 'I always give a lead, go up a ladder first or jump first into any hole. That way I know that I can ask my men to go after me.' Now all that remained for us was to plant the daffodils behind the house and around the parking space.

Unfortunately, however, these activities laid bare the same foundations as existed at the front and the rats now returned and gained access to the walls of the house between the bottom boulders. The problem was that we could not get at the foundation stones to cement in between them because dozens of small stones had been put down to cover the drain. The whole ghastly process began again and I looked with horror at the plaster on the ceilings and wondered how much more of these early morning races the house would withstand. I rigged up a device by my bed, so that I could bang with a hammer with minimum effort and again sought expert advice.

The sanitary inspector arrived and put down gas poison in the rubbish dumps and river banks. We could see the runs but where the rats were coming from remained a mystery and reluctantly I began to use rodein now also illegal. Of all the prevention that we tried this was the most effective, but it was a cruel poison and nerve wracking to use because of the dangers to other animals. One evening a rat arrived by an even more surprising route, entering the walls of the house under the eaves of the one storey kitchen and making a noise like a fluttering bird. There were traces of rat droppings all along the gutter under the tiles, so, although it was nearly dark, I set to work on a cold winter's evening, filling up the large holes under the eaves with cement. This helped to prevent the whistling I was hearing in the evening when a rat would enter from the back or side of the cottage and whistle to its mate who would be entering from the front. Some rat catchers imitate these calls to entice their victims to their death and it is of course the reality behind the fable of the Pied Piper of Hamelin, who played on his pipe until first the rats and then the children followed him out of town. Hearing of our continued plight the sanitary inspector came again and suggested laying half inch mesh rat netting all along the back above the stones, which could be secured to the house and buried on the far side under the bank. At last we had peace. We had denied the rats shelter and they did not return. Occasionally I would see one in the garden and shoot it from my bedroom window, remembering nostalgically that when I came to the cottage I could not even take a mouse from a trap.

Compared with the rats it was impossible not to think of the field mice as our friends. On one occasion in the garden I had a surprising encounter with a tiny brown mouse by the front gate. I suddenly noticed it sitting by a grassy mound planted with daffodils, where it was shovelling grass into its mouth at great speed. I played grandmother's footsteps, creeping up on it, one silent step at a time when it was not looking and then pausing for a minute. At last I only had two steps to go between me and it and I could see it in detail. The little brown mouse was tearing the pieces of grass from the bank with its teeth and then, holding the blade in its hands, was chewing and swallowing it with remarkable rapidity. Immediately one blade was gone it started on another. I could have been looking into a picture book of Beatrice Potter. The mouse appeared quite unconcerned by the tall figure, which by this time was towering above it and blotting out the light. Suddenly it looked up in surprise. 'Great Heavens,' I could imagine it saying. 'What on earth is that?' Nevertheless, it took a few more mouthfuls before it looked again, a longer and more curious look this time. I felt that it was saying on reflection, 'Although this figure keeps so still it might be dangerous. I'd better be off.' It disappeared swiftly down a hole. I waited, feeling I had lost a friend. Then to my astonishment it reappeared and looked at me again as if considering the matter. 'That strange object has still not moved and I do want more grass.' It started eating again with the same rapidity as before, but this time only half its mind was on the job. Instinct had taken over and was telling it to be wary. The trust was broken and the magic gone. A few minutes later it departed never to reappear.

In these remote surroundings humans and animals meet on equal terms. Mrs Anderson, the wife of Robbie, the farmer with the gravel quarry, carries her milking stool and pail to the field and the cow comes and stands to be milked. One day I found her talking to a calf at the roadside. 'Good gracious,' I said, 'I thought I was the only one round here who was daft enough to talk to animals as if they were people.' 'You've got to talk to someone,' was her reply, 'there are nae people here now.' The same thread of affinity and friendship, coupled with a healthy awareness of their destructiveness, binds many country people to the birds. The sound of a peewit's wings beating the air as one steps from one's front door is more agreeable than the roar of a jet aeroplane. Once when I was talking on the telephone a buzzard passed in front of the window, its vast wings outstretched, looking down into the garden for possible prey, while more customary visitors were the herons spotting fish in the burn. Apart from the grouse and birds of prey, whose natural habitat is the hills, and the dippers, which belong to the river, and the snipe, which inhabit the marshes, there are a host of smaller field birds in these upland places, such as hedge sparrows, tits, blackbirds, thrushes, chaffinches, wrens, yellow hammers and pied wagtails. Now like the grouse, these smaller birds are threatened by the protected predators, a protection which is rigorously enforced by eccentrics and governments alike and is resulting in many valuable species, on some of which people depend for their living, being decimated or lost.

Most of these birds were welcome in our garden, but the pigeon was not, for it was the greatest thief of all, although on the whole it was not attracted to our small patch but preferred the larger vegetables of the big house. When my son was nine my brother gave him an air gun, which he particularly chose for its unlethal qualities, but nowhere round the cottage could we find a pigeon at which to aim. We therefore sought the laird's advice and entered unawares into a labyrinthine plot. Apparently an annoying thief was eating his cabbages. We promised help not realising why he did not shoot the pigeon himself. Zilla was shortly to be married and a Spanish couple had been engaged to help with the wedding arrangements. At different times both my cousins had been spotted by the Spaniards carrying guns to shoot the recalcitrant bird. The Spaniards threatened to leave for home if the bird was shot and claimed that pigeons were protected in Spain. Thus John saw a solution in my son's air gun as a scarer not a slayer. Unaware of this we crept up to its favourite tree and there it was, sitting on the top. Hugh fired two near-silent shots. Nothing happened. 'You have a go,' he whispered. By a fluke I shot the pigeon in the head and down it fell. We returned to the kitchen to report success. The Spaniards immediately gave notice and, despite the help of an interpreter who insisted that pigeons were not protected in Spain, they refused to reconsider.

Of all the bird visitors in our garden my favourite was a young curlew, which, just able to fly, coasted in one warm sunny afternoon, when I was gardening. and walked up and down the lawn as if it owned the place and was inspecting our work. I told our Labrador to sit down and perhaps the curlew sensed that she was the quietest dog on earth. We both sat down and the curlew became the only walker in the peace of the garden. Minutes ticked by and then a quarter of an hour. Eventually, wishing to get on with my work, I got up and started trundling the squeaky wheelbarrow round the

Auchmore garden looking north east

garden to collect weeds. The curlew still did not fly away. The Labrador also started patrolling the lawn. Still the curlew did not leave, but, just as I was wondering if it was injured, it rose effortlessly into the air and flew off to its lonely abode in the hills. There is something hauntingly sad about the call and flight of these birds. 'Over the graves of the martyrs,' wrote R.L. Stevenson, 'the whaups are wheeling, my heart remembers how'. Perhaps the young curlew had also sensed this loneliness and realised, 'One is nearer God's heart in a garden than anywhere else on earth'.

4

'There Was no Road'

There is a jingle in the Highlands that runs, 'If you'd seen these roads before they were made, you would lift up your hands and bless General Wade'. Now that we had a house, a car, a garage and a garden we wanted access to it in all weathers – except in deep snow when such a thing was impossible – forgetting that our predecessors had only reached it in a gig. Templeton, the old keeper at Allargue, told a story of life in these hills, which started, 'I went along a road and there was no road...'. The story is forgotten, but these words have become a catch phrase in the family. In the first summer that we were in the cottage we were surrounded by acres of old grass, and when going uphill we were able to turn off the track if it was wet and use the field in order to gain height. This was ideal, because if the wheels started to spin, one could simply turn away from the slope, gain more speed and then try again, possibly not returning to the track until the top. Unfortunately, on our return the following year, we found a fence erected for ploughing and re-seeding, so that there was no room for manoeuvre. We were boxed into the track and the ruts became so deep that I skidded going downhill and nearly hit a post. This would not do, so I collected stones in cardboard boxes and when Bob, my cousin's handyman, arrived with the milk I said, 'I'm going to work on the road this afternoon,' knowing that he, being chivalrous, would reply, 'I'll come and help you.' We made a little improvement, but only to secure the downward journey, so in damp weather the exit had to be on down the hill, round two hairpin bends and over a wooden bridge on to an adopted gravel road.

Then disaster struck. One snowy April night the coal lorry, having failed to make the ascent, stuck fast on the second hairpin bend. With all the courage and stubborn independence of the northern Scot the men refused to telephone for a tractor and together we built a pile of stones and timber to extend the corner and carry the weight of the lorry. Inevitably the flimsy erection gave way at the most perilous moment and the lorry slithered on downhill and came to a stop in the soggy bed of reeds beside the river. We took shelter in the kitchen and drank tea while the tractor was summoned. Rescue work turned out to be extraordinarily difficult and it was nine o'clock and pitch dark before the lorry was extricated. With their black faces wreathed in smiles the coalmen said their evening's work had added years to their lives and brought old age closer. Feeling this innocent statement carried with it the innuendo of a threat – no coal had ever been delivered to the house before, instead it had all been carried by horse or tractor transport – I promised that before I asked them to come again the corner would be enlarged. Knowing that Bob's duodenal ulcer was not suited to this type of work, I took a spade and worked patiently on the hairpin for a week, a little at a time, feeling like a female member of a chain gang in Siberia. I was thinking that I had made a mistake in trying to make a home in such a remote place, whatever the financial or other arguments might be, and there and then I made a promise that at the end of three years I would release myself, unless there was real improvement in the amenities. (Little did I think that we would succeed so far that these three years would be transformed into nearly twenty.) By the end of the week I had managed to cut two or three feet off the upward bank of the second hairpin and in this way our fuel supply was assured.

No sooner, however, had I improved this downhill life-line than another hazard entered our lives. Although technically adopted by the council, the gravelled farm road beyond the bridge only carried traffic to the farm and now that George had moved down the glen the sole users beyond the march (or boundary) fence were ourselves. This lack of regular use now tempted another farmer, who tenanted the fields beyond the march, to use the hillside road fence as part of a sheep pen in which to sort his sheep. On two occasions I slithered through the mud and round the corners to meet hundreds of sheep penned in behind heavy gates on the road. On the first occasion I waited a long time, on the second I decided on impulse to release the sheep, being already pressed for time for an appointment. I heard shouts behind me but kept going. The two rules, if you live 'outbye', are never to let out stock, and if you find them wandering either return them or get a message to the owner. By letting out sheep on purpose I had committed an unforgivable sin, but fortunately I found an ally in the roadman who took his boss on a wordless walk along the adopted road on a day when these activities were again in operation. When the farmer met me again he said, 'You'd nae need to report me.' 'I did not officially report you,' I replied and did not give away my accomplice, but he must have known that the origin of the leak was myself. It was decades before our relationship was restored to normality and I could feel that I had been forgiven. We do not fall out with each other in this glen except when survival is threatened, but if we do it takes a 'wee while' for normal relations to be restored.

The trouble is that we all break rules when it suits us as I found to my advantage, with the roadman turning out to be a very useful ally in other respects. The surface of our downward route was now so bad that I was continually breaking shock absorbers. The roadman therefore came across one afternoon to help and made a diplomatic approach down the council road, sweeping leaves with a brush. In this way he hoped that he would disguise the fact that he was going to give me a hand on the wrong side of the wooden bridge. First we dug out and rolled away the boulders that came up underneath the car, then we laid big stones in the ruts and soft places and later smaller stones and gravel from the burn on the top of these. He was an artist at his job and lost himself in impassioned discourses on the principles and technicalities of road making. But our work was swept away in the winter, for when I returned in the spring I found that a combination of tractor and livestock had once more removed all traces of the surface. It had simply sunk from sight. 'Waste of time,' said George, the farmer, whose fields surrounded us. 'I've poured cartloads of stones into it and had to give up.' Gazing at the muddy waste before me I believed him. Despair stared me in the face.

Worse, however, was to come. One warm June night lime was delivered on the wrong side of the burn and giant lorries crossed and recrossed the wooden bridge until it disintegrated. Simultaneously the weather broke and the gas man arrived in a lorry delivering bottled gas. My son, who previously had been either too small or at school at times of crises with the road, lent a hand and it took the three of us two hours to get the lorry back up the hill, using sacks, spades, gravel and boulders on a night of pouring rain such as only the north of Scotland provides. Tempers were in danger of running high – 'Why,' asked the driver testily, 'did you not tell us that the bridge was broken?' He was probably unaware that less than half a century ago such excitement was commonplace in these parts, for the road over the hill was only tarmacadamed in 1933. Before that date cars stuck regularly on the steep gradients and had to be pushed up – through mud made deeper by motor bike trials – requiring, as the gas lorry had done, supporting boulders under the wheels with each tiny movement upwards. The children of lairds, farmers and keepers were only too happy then to carry on the tradition described in *Boswell's Journal of a Tour to the Hebrides* of boys and girls collecting tips from travellers in return for help with their carriages. In those days the road over the hill was a succession of hairpin bends, and, although this was less strain on the engine going up, the corners were difficult to negotiate going down, if foolhardy drivers burnt out their brakes by not using their gears. In one such accident during the war an armoured personnel carrier went out of control, nose diving into a 'bothy' on the last hairpin bend, where the sudden drop in floor level saved it from crashing through the hotel beyond. We had ourselves now learnt the danger of steep muddy bends on the downward journey when our car had slithered out of control; and had also experienced the strain on tempers on the upward slope, when, with helpers pushing, sacks insulating tyres from the mud and the driver gentle with the throttle, a valuable inch was gained, only to be lost again, because there was no boulder ready to be slipped under a wheel. As with the coal delivery I had to promise not to order gas again until either the bridge was repaired or the upward track improved.

Before we had time to decide on the next course of action I had a good offer for my twelve year old car and bought a new small estate van. Although backed by Dod Massie, one of the best motor engineers in the north of Scotland – a man of great integrity who, in the words of the schoolmistress, 'was not heavy on the pencil' – I was not going to risk this on the downward route. Clearly this was our Waterloo. Either I must find a solution to the upward route, which had the advantage of not being used by tractors, or pack and go. Cut into the side of the bank, the grassy track above us led down from a gate to the cottage, which stood about three quarters of the way down to the burn. The grass was high in the middle, flanked by deep muddy grassy ruts on either side. Kind friends were free with advice: 'If you can get a run at it you will be all right. What you want to do is to make a track joining your gate with the track going past you'. So I ordered a load of granite chips from the quarry over the hill to come only on a dry day and asked Doddie Coutts, another farmer – who, being a younger brother, had time to spare for outside work – to bring a plough. He was a charming fellow, who had been badly wounded in the war, and he brought a bag of pan drops with him 'to maintain morale'. He also brought a ready wit. Early in the desert campaign he had been given CB for writing a letter home saying, 'There are no Field Marshalls here, only field mice.' Now there were four of us at work – my son, a girl student, Doddie and myself – and by the end of the day we had succeeded in cutting a deep path through the grass to connect up the track with the front gate. With the aid of the chips which we spread over the cutting and on the parking place (previously made with the soil from the back of the house) we could get a run at the hill. It worked splendidly in the summer, but again, once autumn came, one's wheels on the main part of the track spun as hopelessly as before. Still in a 'do or die' mood I therefore ordered gravel for the road from Robbie, the farmer with the local gravel quarry, who had helped with the bank behind the house. He came next day while I was out and laid gravel on the steepest part of the track but unfortunately it was spread too thick, contained too many big stones and needed rolling, so that my first experience was to stick going downhill and to have to dig out large boulders from under the car in order to get home. The gloom of a November night did nothing to cheer my spirits. I was beginning to think that I had had enough!

The position was clearly desperate. Although the following morning the rain was like a monsoon, I nevertheless sallied forth and collected Doddie, who was just on his way inside to a seat by the fire – the only place to be on such a day – and Robbie, the gravel spreader, who was full of apologies and kindly said he would give me a morning's work free of charge because he knew he had spread the surface too thick. While the two men worked with tractor and trailer, removing surplus gravel on the steepest part of the track nearest to the cottage and taking it to barer places, I went further up and started digging off the sods of grass. To my amazement a road appeared made of hard stones about eight inches below the present surface. Between us and sustained by Doddie's pan drops, a morning's work produced fifty yards of skinned surface, which we then covered with gravel. Days later, with broken backs and having received more cartloads of gravel, the whole road was up to the standard of the first fifty yards. Now it was a proper road once more, as it had obviously been at one time. It was not a track any longer.

I went home that night to my fireside and pictured in my mind how once the Highland roads had been. First, they were heather tracks over which horses pulled sledge carts. Then the 'drove' roads took the cattle – and later the sheep – to market and to winter pasture over tracks worn bare with marching feet. Many of these became public highways in the modern world. Others were accepted as rights of way; others lapsed and became extinct. After the Union of Crowns, public responsibility for roads was legally placed by a 1669 Act of Parliament upon the shoulders of the Justices of the Peace, who were given power to demand six day's labour with a horse on the roads each year from all parish residents. The heritors were to be rated on the land they owned, which would make a contribution to the building of roads and bridges, with turnpikes suitably placed to demand payment by users. After the 1715 Rebellion General Wade was sent to Scotland to start a programme of road building and this was as much to open up and bring economic progress to the country as to quell further revolt by means of a military presence. In all Wade built thirty five bridges himself, using William Adam, the famous Scottish architect, for the more ambitious spans.

The Wade Bridge on the old military road

Like the Romans, Wade went straight through obstructions; two thousand yards of solid rock did not deter him. His roads on average were sixteen feet wide: thirty in the south going down to ten in the north. Boulders in the way were raised with jacks and spikes and rolled to one side to mark the way. Just as the road man had done on the track below the cottage, smaller rocks were put into holes which were dug beside them. But whereas we had added the boulders to the muddy soil, Wade's men dug out every particle of soft soil from boggy ground before filling the hollow with layers of large stones, adding sometimes the trunks of trees, and then smaller stones with up to three feet of gravel on the top to form a smooth and binding surface. When roads traversed slopes as our top track did, then a cutting was made into the hill rather than building up the road on the down side. By the time the military roads were extended to the eastern foothills of the Cairngorms, the Turnpike Act of 1751 was assessing farmers and lairds alike, asking them to subscribe in equal proportions to the building and maintenance of public roads. By the end of the eighteenth century the direct labour force on the military roads had been discontinued and repair work was put out to contract until 1812, when Parliament gave Commissioners of Supply the duty of keeping up the military roads still in use. These Commissioners, together with the heritors and JPs maintained and constructed public roads in the Highlands under Acts of 1803 and 1804 until the Local Government Act was passed in 1889, putting road maintenance on a modern footing. This was the period during which the Luib Bridge in Corgarff was gifted by Sir Charles Forbes, while his son built bridges at Newe and Buchaarn in Strathdon out of funds left by his great uncle, John of Bombay. Throughout the nineteenth century, following the techniques pioneered by Wade, gravelled roads were built in Deeside and Donside, some of which led miles up into the hills to what are now ruined villages. Once on a picnic in Deeside we had followed such a road five or six miles into the hills where we could see the stony remains of a large deserted village. Coming to a locked gate we had congratulated ourselves on circumnavigating it through a group of trees only to discover on our return that the keeper had erected an instant fence and was lying in wait for us, fortunately in good humour.

My evening of reflection by the fire ended to the sound of pouring rain. Before I had a chance to use my car wheels to roll the gravel flat – the old bottoming was still slippery with earth and residues of turf, and the gravel had not bound – it started to downpour and three days of heavy rain washed so much mud back on to the road that it took another week of patiently sorting the mud from the gravel with spade and bare hands and then rolling it with the car wheels section by section before the road was really firm. Now the only danger was from the occasional tractor, but given any luck this might be harmless once the surface was really hard. In admiration for my labours kind Doddie refused any payment for his final day's work, 'You've had enough expense with the road already.'

For nearly fifteen years we had no trouble. Then for some reason the bank on the burn side of the downward track began to crumble. We had no cause now to use it and sadly our days at the cottage were numbered, for

COCKBRIDGE AND THE MOUNTAIN ROAD TO TOMINTOUL   AIOII

The old Lecht road

we had bought a house elsewhere. Nevertheless, I felt that, as a gesture of thanks and a help to a young married cousin, who was going to use the cottage for weekends, we would get a local contractor to do the job before we left. He took a long time to come and, without any thought, I ordered coal which would arrive on a lorry using the top track. It rained and rained before they came and the men who delivered the coal were the same two who had drunk tea in the cottage and waited for the tractor nearly twenty years before. To my horror they had brought a new broader lorry and said they had scraped the sides coming through the gate and could not go back without doing further damage because the steep run-up meant they would have to go through the gate at speed. In trepidation I took them to see the downward track. The fence hung crazily in mid air over the hole in the track at the top of the steep bank. 'Oh, we'll manage that,' they said cheerfully, 'we'll take it fairly fast.' I remembered the dark night twenty years earlier and my heart sank. But they seemed determined. 'Shall I come?' I asked. 'No,' they replied, 'Just pray.' I went back into the garden and did just that. When I looked up again I saw the lorry re-appearing at the bottom of the hill and watched it safely cross the bridge and disappear into the distance. 'Oatmeal,' Dr Samuel Johnson is reported as saying, 'is a food for horses in England and for men in Scotland.' 'Ah,' returned Boswell, 'but where else, Sir, would you find such horses or such men.'

5

Postie

When I moved into the cottage in the early fifties Britain was still in the throes of post-war austerity and there was no hope of a telephone. Because infants become ill suddenly, kind parents, encouraged by anxious relations and friends, fitted an electric bell up to the big house, which was carried on small telephone posts (used by the Post Office a few years later to put in a party line). Until then the only regular communication with the outside world was John Reid, the postie, who brought not only letters but the newspaper and (independently of regulations and only in a crisis) parcels from the local shop. He also took away non-urgent letters in his post bag. We only used the electric bell twice, once when it went off by mistake and once when, after a storm, it failed to work. Otherwise postie was our life line – no help that he could give was ever withheld. As well as farming and fencing in his spare time, he was one of the leading pipers in the Lonach pipe band and sometimes in the evening the haunting strains of pipe music wafted across the glen. His daily journey included a two mile bicycle ride up the drive of the shooting lodge on the southern bank of the river, coming back over a swing wooden foot bridge, up the steps of which he carried his bicycle, and the same distance over grass and rough track on the northern bank, calling on the few outlying cottages and farms. As if this was not enough he also as an obligement swept chimneys. 'There's no charge for sweeping chimneys,' was his invariable reply to questions of cost and one then enquired as to his favourite brands of cigarettes or tobacco. The knowledge that once a day someone would call removed the worst feelings of isolation, for, apart from Sundays, the only days he did not come were when the snow plough could not reach the sub post office or when there was a blizzard and blind drift at the head of the glen. A year after our arrival John Reid retired. Having known him since wartime days this left a gap, but he was always to be found in his croft a mile away, looked after by his devoted and excellent wife, a retired school mistress of great intelligence, who sold chickens and eggs and taught Hugh German when he was away from school on account of a broken leg.

The sub post office, to which the red mail van then came, was also a shop. Overhead the pylons carried the power away to the cities, but owing to the cost of transformers they could not supply electric light to the head of the glen and within the shop's cosy brown varnished interior a paraffin lamp swung from the ceiling to light the wide counters and stone-flagged floor. In those days Lottie the postmistress also operated the local telephone exchange with great efficiency, the only problem being that if she was out with her hens one had to wait until she returned. Later an automatic exchange was installed across the road. To begin with it was out of order whenever there was a blizzard, but as the years went by it became quick and efficient. By the time we came to live in the glen there were not a great number of things you could buy in the shop, just imperishable foodstuffs, such as chocolate, biscuits, syrup and tea.

Now the postmistress' husband, Jimmy Niven, took the job of postie. He sorted the mail which came up on the post van and set off on his rounds, pushing his bicycle over the hill tracks and riding it on the bottomed gravel roads. During the winter storms he wore a woolly hat with ear-flaps, and changed his bicycle for a shepherd's crook, in case he found a sheep in trouble, and was often himself up to his waist in snowdrifts. All sorts of parcels came up on the van without the knowledge of the GPO, and normally these had to be collected from the post office because of the weight on his bicycle. They were mostly groceries, but sometimes other things besides. Occasionally an inspector would ride with the postie driver from Strathdon to make sure that nothing was carried illegally in this way. One morning Jimmy Philip, the postie driver, met me coming into the post office to get a parcel. Usually when he had an inspector with him he would alert me with a wink or a nod. This time the inspector was already in the shop and so he blocked my entrance with his bulky figure and then took me round the back of the shop to deliver into my hands the clandestine parcel. On another occasion circumstances became yet more tricky, but mercifully the inspector feigned deafness or genuinely did not hear. By that time my son was six and ready to remind his mother. 'Where is the oatmeal?' he chirruped. 'We're going to Mrs Reid for that,' I replied, mentioning the name of the ex-postie's wife where we got our eggs, trying to indicate by sign language that there was danger around. 'But we never get oatmeal from Mrs Reid,' he continued, thinking his mother had temporarily gone daft. I did not know what to do – eventually the inspector would come out of his reverie and the fat would be in the fire. So, taking Hugh by the back of his coat collar, I literally dragged him out of the shop, his heels trundling over the flag stones, still talking about oatmeal.

Our new postie was also the local mole-catcher and he would arrive in the evening when his work was done to set the traps. Like the last postie he would accept no money, just toffee or ten cigarettes. I had come to realise that it was in fact very difficult to press money on anyone in the glen. Everyone liked to think that they could help each other for nothing and it was deeply generous. 'There's no charge', meant that a present would be preferred. 'I'll get it again', meant that money would be accepted, but that time was no object. Sometimes when a kindness had been done a bottle of whisky was the answer, sometimes only a nip of whisky; sometimes tobacco or sweeties were preferred. The acceptance of money was an embarrassment to the recipient and it was part of Highland courtesy to help the giver also to forget the transaction.

It was a very great disappointment to the glen when our postie was laid off after a threatened strike of post office workers. The authorities decided that they would save the money required for higher wages by replacing the postmen in outlying districts with landrovers operated from main post offices. When this change was first made the mail was delivered an hour earlier in summer, but in winter, if the landrover could not get through, one or two outlying places cut off by snowdrifts were not visited at all and they had to fetch their own mail or wait for a better day. Furthermore, owing to the new schedule, outgoing letters did not arrive at the main post office in time to catch the mid-day bus and the train going south, so that Saturday being a half day it was impossible to send a letter from the glen between Friday and Monday – such was the nature of progress.

When the shiny red landrover arrived in the village, postie was therefore out of work. He did gardening jobs to help out so I knew that he would like to give us a hand. He wore his old uniform every day, carried his tools in his postman's bag, and finished his working day with the familiar words, 'Well, I'll need to be getting on down the road', whereas before it had always been, 'Well, I'll need to be getting on up the road'. When by May, the gardens were all cultivated the only full time job he could find was a heavy one with the Forestry Commission. He is a small, slightly built man, not very robust with a duodenal ulcer, but if you asked him or his wife how he was the answers were always the same, 'Fine' or 'No complaints'. There never are.

No sooner had we adjusted to the new system than the sub post office itself was threatened with closure. A meeting was called in the local town to discuss the matter, but no one from the glen attended. The people of the north east are too proud to ask for favours and so economic with words in their speech that they are not over-confident of winning a case without help in presentation. They are also too proud to complain and too gentlemanly; rather than argue they would give you the chairs on which they are sitting. They prefer to let their thoughts wander down stream and over the hills. 'Have you seen my plants,' says the postmistress in order to change a controversial subject; 'There's a salmon lying yonder at the bridge,' says her husband if you ask too many questions; 'Look, John, there's a big fat thrush in the garden,' says Mrs Reid, the wife of the ex-postie, who is asleep by the fire; that is all the response you will get if you try to persuade anyone to take a stand against the march of bureaucracy. This is not altogether a polite way of asking you not to interfere, but rather a lack of self-interest and a sense of hopelessness that the world does not understand the plight of the depopulated upland areas and is not sufficiently interested to learn the reasons for it. After all if you do not fight you cannot be defeated. These people count their spiritual integrity above the possession of worldly goods and find lost causes sweeter than battling for selfish ends.

Nevertheless, when it comes to survival the glen is able, through subterfuge, to pull a number of chestnuts from the fire. When the test week came and records were taken everyone knew well in advance and people came from far and wide with letters, parcels and telegrams so that the takings were high and the sub post office was spared. The usual time table is that first the churches are consolidated; then the post office is closed; then the school; finally, like migrating birds, the last inhabitants dwindle away to join the flock and heather creeps down over once cultivated fields. For the moment the crisis had been averted. Chocolate, biscuits, syrup and tea were still sold over the wide counters of the shop and I could continue as heretofore to occasionally post a letter in the box and write in the place where the postage stamp goes, 'No stamps. Please stamp. Pay tomorrow'. Once a week the postmistress still bought all the bread for the village, wrapped it in newspaper and put it on a high shelf for collection and if the carrier left a parcel of plants late on Saturday night we could be sure that she or her husband would bring them two miles on a Sunday rather than let them spoil. In the struggle for existence everyone in this glen has learnt to be good neighbours one with another.

Indeed, even the animals were relieved that the shop and sub post office had been saved. The postmistress had two cats and many chickens and our Labrador was always given a biscuit every time we paid her a visit. When we later came to have ponies they also knew to turn in off the road to the shop entrance on their own initiative and, although the postmistress, being a little fearful of horses, gave them oatcakes at a discreet distance, they all quickly put her on their visiting list and saw her as a favourite person. The first pony we had, being mostly Shetland and therefore small, followed us into the post office one day. It happened before the landrover was put on and we were delivering mail to catch the night train. Trying to follow us in through one side of the double doors, he got his head and shoulders so far through that it seemed easier to open the other door and let him come in in order to turn him round. Once inside he had to have his ritual oatcake, and, hearing the van approach, we shut the door again. Postie arrived, flung open the door and met a pony, head first, 'My, fit's that you've got here? A horse?'

Jock Philip the postie with his landrover

No sooner had the landrover arrived, driven by Jimmy Philip's son Jock, than we realised that we had an even better life line to the outside world. As with the previous vehicle, regulations of those days forbade posties

41

carrying anything but mail, but as before no regulations were strictly adhered to and this time we had door to door delivery. Both the posties from the village down the strath were renowned for their wit and they brought us news and gossip from a wider world. Legislation regarding sale of milk had been under way for some time and in order to stamp out tuberculosis it was becoming more stringent. Soon we were made to purchase our milk from an accredited dairy eight miles away instead of from over the river. The bottles came up with the post, but unfortunately the estate on the south bank of the river, which had been bought by people from England, used the same source of supply and in their case it was a churn. Someone reported the posties and there was great consternation. The supply was stopped and there was a meeting in the far away town to which the post mistress and the posties were bidden. The post mistress said she would not attend, and, although I offered to help in any way I could with evidence and excuses for the breach, the matter was met with true Highland prevarication and was quietly allowed to drop. When I asked the post mistress what the posties were going to do about my supply of milk she replied in astonishment, 'What are they going to do? They're going to go on carrying it of course'. In this way our life line was spared, parcels continued to arrive as before and the glen breathed a sigh of relief. Soon, as more estate owners and farmers acquired snow ploughs for the tractors, the landrover's scope in winter widened; probably it would not be long before our isolation was ended and we would be encroached upon by the long arm of suburbia.

Then, to everyone's sadness, the postmistress retired, the sub post office and shop were closed and the house sold. She and her husband moved a little further down the glen, so that he had a longer bicycle ride when he came to the gardens or to take the pony to the hill to carry the panniers for the grouse. Without the landrover the closure of the post office would have been a disaster, but the wonderful spirit of the Strathdon posties and the splendid organisation of Shand's shop again allowed the glen to survive. Although once a week a butcher and a fish man called at the houses on the main road, they did not go to as many outlying farms and cottages as the travelling shop from Strathdon. We were fortunate in that all the time we were in the cottage Sandy Shand arrived in Corgarff on Friday with his van, which took most of the day to go round the head of the glen and carried almost everything. Without his efficient and dedicated service we would never have survived. If something was not on the van Sandy would get it on his weekly visit to town and deliver it with my groceries to the big house,

Lady Forbes with Jimmy Niven at the Post Office

which was our collection point. A German boy, who was staying with us to improve his English, was amazed to see lights in the shop at one a.m. on our way back from a dance and to be welcomed as shoppers at this hour. Once a year I received an account hand-written into a red exercise book.

There was an unspoken rule that anyone going down the road would bring up a parcel or a newspaper from the shop addressed to someone else and either deliver it or leave it at the hotel, for even with a car distances are so great in remote areas that no one can afford the time or petrol to fetch individual items from so many miles away. The fact is that you cannot have public transport if there not enough people to use it and without transport you are unlikely to have sufficient people in the glens. Not long after the war Agnes made great efforts to get a weekly bus to run the last eight miles up the road. Meeting it one evening to collect a parcel and seeing that it had no passengers, she said to Ian McDonald, the hotelier and farm grieve, 'But there's no one in it.' 'There's never naebody in it,' was the double negative reply and shortly afterwards it was taken off again.

It is because of this lack of transport, the long distances covered and the remoteness of neighbour from neighbour that the posties have throughout history taken on such an important role in the life of Scottish rural communities. In England it was the mail coach that formed the focus of attention for artists and historians, but for centuries in the Highlands, whether deliveries were by boat, gig, pony, bicycle, van, on foot or by landrover it was the postie himself who took on this role. 'Tell them not to worry,' is his message to all newcomers anxious about the problems of remoteness, 'for the postie aye calls.'

6

Mountain and Moorland Ponies

Horses are in my blood on the maternal side and almost all my life I have had something to ride. They are after all the oldest form of transport – in W.H. Ogilvie's words, 'The ghosts that hold for ever the highway of the years'. I therefore wanted the same for Hugh and I thought perhaps a cart would be useful also. Three years after we moved in I bought a pony for him, a cross-Shetland which would have won a first in a class known locally as 'roadsters'. I advertised in the local newspaper but replies were either unsuitable or expensive, except for one which said, 'We have a grey white Shetland Welsh horse pony for sale. £20'. This seemed Double Dutch, for I did not yet know that 'horse' in local terminology means gelding, nor had I seen a skewbald that was grey and white, but I knew by instinct when I saw the pony that Welsh was his least likely cross-breeding. His name was Dusty and it suited him, for to match his colouring he had two impenetrable half-white wall eyes which made it disconcertingly difficult to read his inner thoughts, which were usually wicked. Although he was larger than the average Shetland he had inherited the cunning, obstinacy and independence of this ancient breed.

Surrounded as we were by unfenced acres of hill grass and heather I was relieved to hear that he had been tethered and to be given the swivel and peg that the sellers threw in with the price. These render it almost impossible for an animal to tie itself up in a rope and damage a fetlock. The problem of how to get him home was quickly solved. 'We'll send him in with the cattle to the mart and you can find a lorry taking beasts in your direction'. By the time we arrived and before we had found Dusty tied up among the cattle a Shetland dealer had found us and offered more than our price. Pleased by his interest I explained that after my long search I could not let him go. Back home, it was just getting dark when we heard the sound of trotting hooves outside the window. They were like music to my ears as I realised that the china horses on the shelf in the dining room had once more come to life. Within minutes Dusty was securely fixed to his tether behind the house and was quietly grazing. Or so we thought.

Time was to show that secure was never the word to be applied to anything by which Dusty was retained. This wall eyed ruffian could undo any clip attached to his halter, although it was reinforced with string or wire and was fixed directly behind his chin out of reach of his teeth. He seemed capable of conjuring tricks. Half an hour after leaving him he was gone, up the hill or into the marsh, although luckily he was home loving and only out of sight when we had visitors and wanted no distractions. It was the same with the gate to the tiny holding field on two sides of the garden. He would watch while we tied knots and then he had a little sleep. This was essential for the functioning of his brain. When we looked out there he was innocently snoozing. Then, when he awoke and no one was watching, he untied all the knots with his teeth and opened the gate. Even a bolt on a gate dropped on its hinges did not deter him. The shepherd at the home farm once recounted how he found him lifting a gate with his teeth and knocking the bolt along with his knee. Some time later I met the shepherd on the road and told him I had used this story in a book I was writing about our ponies. 'That's nae a story,' he replied, hurt, 'that's true.'

With a brain like a bank robber, Dusty was useless as a child's pony, except on the leading rein. Sometimes I, or the student I had helping me in the summer vacation, rode him to keep him in order and, resenting our weight, he tried to rush to the nearest fence to scrape one's knee against a post in a vain attempt to get one off. However, he served his turn, provided there was always an adult at his head and soon Hugh was riding to school with me running alongside. We could now go on longer expeditions over the hills and at pulling a cart Dusty was splendid. The cart was a present from my cousins. The blacksmith fixed a bent axle, a kind friend sold me harness and we were able to have frequent picnics with numerous children piled into the cart, thinking they were driving the pony when in fact we were running alongside to steer them from disaster. It was extraordinary that a pony so contrary in the saddle could be so obedient in a cart. In photographs we looked like travelling folk, but not so long ago horse transport was the norm in the glen. I had ridden to the cottage in a gig in the war and as a child had travelled in a grocer's gig elsewhere in the Highlands, where the son of the shop drove a weekly delivery service far up into the hills.

As the nights drew in it became important to find a home for Dusty in the winter when we would be away. 'I'll have naethin' to dae with him in the winter, mind,' warned George, who kindly gave us grazing and refused to take payment or presents except a bottle of whisky at New Year. Enquiries received the same answer, particularly from the grieve who ran the home farm and hotel and looked after the Allargue Highland mare and two foals. At last I found friends who said they would have him. Triumphant I went into the hotel kitchen to break the good news. 'You should just ask Ian,' said his wife, stirring porridge. 'But he has always said he would not take him,' I replied. 'You should just ask him,' she repeated in the same placid tone. When I found him in the byre and reminded him of our earlier discussions he said laconically, 'Nane o' them hae shoes on. They canna dae themselves nae harm.' He spoke as though this was the first time the matter had been discussed and I realised that the north east Scot does not want to have his kindness presumed. Only when you have your load on your back will everyone say, 'Here, give it to me.'

During the first winter Dusty behaved himself, but during the second he fell into the frozen river. Whether this was caused by his mania for exploration or whether, cocksure as ever, he mistook a pile of snow for the river bank remained his secret. He had stood with me earlier in the year on the edge of the water watching a digger deepening the bed and only when, amazed at his fearlessness, I altered my stance and put him between me and the juggernaut did he think he was too close for comfort. He was a brave rebel who trusted human judgement in matters of personal safety. Whatever the reason in seconds he was plunging in the icy black water with men running for ropes. His rescue had to be from the far bank and, the snow remaining for weeks too deep to move him, this meant that he had to be specially fed. His health was affected and the next winter – even in a milder climate further down the strath – he had pneumonia. Offered a good price from a farmer who knew his weakness we took it thankfully. We had enjoyed his individuality, courage and native cunning, but we said goodbye without regret and started the search for a more suitable pony.

At that time there was little recreational riding in the north of Scotland. Pony trekking caught the public imagination later. Highland ponies – or garrons – were used on the hill carrying grouse in panniers or stags slung over in special harness, but many of these had been crossed at some time with Clydesdales and were little use as riding ponies for children. The lighter Eriskay ponies had not yet appeared in any numbers and so there was a gap which could only be filled by importing native breeds from further south, which for us meant finding winter accommodation elsewhere. Following this quest I set off on holiday in the early spring to Wales, Exmoor and Dartmoor. I had not been to Wales before and fell in love with the soft mountain scenery and the houses and farms perched half way up the valleys. After the sterner and colder rocky barrenness of the Highlands primroses among the grass in early March were a balm to the soul. I did not need to go further than the valley of the River Usk before finding fields of Welsh mountain mares and foals with perfect heads and wise prominent eyes. 'Don't give them corn, though,' the local people warned, 'goes to their heads at once.' There are three distinct breeds: the small Welsh mountain, the larger Welsh pony and the stocky Welsh cob. I rode a quiet and gentle Welsh cob mountain cross, easy to go and stop and sure footed as a mountain goat. A child of six could have ridden her, although she was up to an adult's weight. 'How much will you take for her,' I asked. 'Nothing,' was the reply, 'she's worth all the money in the world to me with the trekking and the school.'

Still unsuited, therefore, I set off again for the rocky outcrops and steep valleys of Exmoor, but it was as difficult there to find anyone breeding Exmoors as it had been to avoid Welsh pony breeders in Wales. 'They're far too strong for children,' I was warned, 'and they're obstinate as mules.' I persevered nevertheless and soon was being given a leg up on to a four year old Exmoor thoroughbred cross, strong and springy with a long easy stride, which I rode up on to the moor with a member of a family who had bred Exmoors for generations. Here we found the herd of mares and a perfect little stallion who came and talked to us, nose to nose. It seemed inconceivable that he and my grey half-bred could have been father and son, so quickly do the pony characteristics fall away. What tremendous chests these sturdy ponies have, what wonderful head carriages and depth through the heart, all of which carry on through generations of crossed blood, whereas the mealie nose, distinguishing mark of the breed, disappears in two. But they are too strong for small children and too nervous, a nervousness which it is said springs from distrust of humans learnt during their early days in this wild spell-bound country of Lorna Doone.

On I went to the barren openness of Dartmoor where I tore across the heather on a diminutive Dartmoor pony which gathered itself under me like a coiled spring in the way I remembered so well from the days of my youth, when I learnt to ride on a dark bay Dartmoor pony remarkable for its fleetness of foot. These ponies can keep up with thoroughbreds over a short distance, but their very keenness and speed can make them upsetting for a child unless they are well broken. The New Forest, where my parents had a house, was my last port of call. Here the mares and foals are rounded up in autumn 'drifts' after which the colts are sold unless they escape their mounted pursuers or are passed by the Verderers as stallions. These ponies have wonderfully long strides and beautiful head carriages, thoroughbreds having run in the Forest in Queen Victoria's time. They also have steady temperaments, but they are too large for young children, so instead I found there what I was looking for, a grey Welsh mountain called Seagull. He was ideal, except, as we were warned, he had been bogged in the Forest when hunting and broke into a lather of fear whenever he saw hounds or heard the horn.

Hugh on Seagull

That was not likely to bother us in northern Scotland and so I bought a two-wheeled pony trailer, fixed it up behind my small A35 van and set off with my son and an intrepid friend who insisted we learnt to reverse. This was provident for there were problems ahead. In Yorkshire the pony started to stamp. I swung him on the corners to persuade him to keep his feet but to no avail. Unboxing him by the roadside we were joined by an engaging tramp who had his lunch in the proverbial red spotted handkerchief. 'Put him in the other way round so that he can see out,' he advised. By curious coincidence we were only a mile or two away from an estate where the owner employed as factor Edward Wilson of the Antarctic's brother who had married a cousin of ours. His employer habitually dressed in very shabby clothes and one day fell into conversation with a tramp leaning on a gate. 'Do you belong hereabouts?' asked the tramp. 'Well I suppose in a manner of speaking you could say that hereabouts belongs to me,' came the humorous reply. We all settled down to a convivial lunch together after which we took the tramp's advice. Seagull travelled with his head out all the way to Scotland and in this manner he continued to travel for the rest of his time with us.

A new vista now opened before us, for there were around us many paths and tracks which could be explored leading to kirks, schools, peat bogs and springs and linking main thoroughfares. Some were mere grants, others were rights of way, requiring use for twenty years which must not have lapsed for more than twenty. Rights of way have not recently been so well defined or rigorously upheld in Scotland as in England, because in Scotland the law of trespass is based on proven damage, whereas in England the threat of damage to the person or to property is sufficient to found an action. Some of these tracks are footpaths or bridleways, others are drove roads dating from days when drovers took their cattle and later sheep to the markets at Crieff and Falkirk. Originally many of the cattle were thieved, but after the 1745 Rebellion the whole trade became lawful, the price of cattle trebled and prosperous owners rode ponies or used pack horses on routes which lay across mountain passes and ridges and down glens, where the cattle swam the rivers. Their stories are immortalised in Sir Walter Scott's true story of *The Two Drovers.* The boom in black cattle ended in the first half of the nineteenth century, by which time the sheep had started to arrive after an increase in the price of wool, and this was simultaneous with the roads becoming too circumscribed to provide pasture, railways beginning and auctioneers travelling to smaller trysts. By the time the slower droving of sheep began bridges had been built and the sheep were often merely moving to winter pastures. Although grazing rights along the way were put in jeopardy after a House of Lords decision later in the nineteenth century, rights of way were not disputed and in the early twentieth century actions for trespass fade from the pages of the *Scots Law Times.*

Many of these paths and tracks round us went up one burn to the source and down another, linking two straths and villages without going over the tops amid the winter snows. Others were old military roads, others again led to lochs and homesteads with a double entrance linking two highways. In the remote Highlands courtesy is endemic and even if a right of passage is secure anyone walking or taking a pony across another's land will give warning that they are coming. Until the motor car brought urban dwellers to the countryside there were thus no difficulties about access. No one walked on moors during the shooting season, either of grouse or red deer, and to balance that deference few landowners locked gates. It is claimed that problems began when absentee landlords, whose woods were open to riders and walkers on their English estates, were tempted by remoteness to make their own rules north of the Border and the position was then exacerbated by the court's interpretation of an occupier's liability when child trespassers, injured by machinery left lying about, were able to successfully sue for damages. Many public spirited landowners tried to restrict access after that decision, where previously their land had been open. We were fortunate in that these matters barely touched us – indeed round us keepers were so generous that some would tell us a route was marked when, even lying on the heather, one could still not see it bent by wheels or feet. In these circumstances, when a track petered out, only patience kept one out of bogs and reliance on the large soup plate feet of my cousin's Highland mare, which were the best defence when seeking a way through the labyrinth of potentially treacherous tracks.

With Seagull outgrown and sold to friends, who promised never to part with him, Hugh rode the New Forest pony that I bought as a three year old for myself to ride. Like a number of youngsters from the Forest he did not like anything pressing upon the top of his head, for these colts are caught in the 'drifts', haltered to trees and branded, so that later, unable to communicate their fear to humans, some jib when led in hand and get a bad name. Rufus came to us from a dealer thin and covered with fleas, but – our patience tried to the limit – we persisted and, with advice from Forest friends, drove him on from behind on a long rein whenever he stopped. He then attached himself to us with an endearing loyalty that inspired me to turn from article writing to writing a children's book about a pony with his problems. When Seagull arrived from his winter home and found Rufus installed behind the electric fence, which had replaced the tether, they fought like stallions until separated, so the following spring we put the larger pony in with the smaller one and, possession adding inches to stature, the jousting stakes were levelled and peace reigned. When Seagull went I bought a young Fell for myself whose mother had killed herself on a fence when bolting from lightening in a thunderstorm. The pony was a good mover, well proportioned and up to weight but it should have occurred to us that the reason the price was cheap was because the sellers suspected that it was a case of like mother like son. There was a daftness in his head, for his eyes flashed dark red when he was annoyed and he had to be exhausted by lunging before the smith could get shoes on him. I did not allow anyone else to ride him, but he was easy to break and reasonably well behaved. Then one day he caught his bit for a moment in a fence when I was opening a gate and if Agnes, riding with me, had not shouted 'Get off' I would have been carried through the half open gate, bolted with along the drive, over or through a wire fence and under the low branches of fir trees. His bridle was broken and the saddle damaged but he came home contrite of his own accord and I rode him regularly through the summer, selling him at a sale with no warranty except that he was strong and sound. It was then that we bought a comfortable Highland to replace the Allargue mare who had died and she worked on the hill for my cousins during the first two weeks of the shooting season, being ours for the rest of the year. 'Her name is Dorothy,' said Charlie Gordon, the carrier, to his son on the telephone when asking him to collect her, 'and she's nae a girl.' But in fact she was very feminine in all her ways and could be trusted to stop Rufus eating the flowers when on occasions we had been too busy to mow the lawn and required a quick cut. Before we left the cottage we made longer expeditions into the mountains with my son and his friends, some riding, some walking in relays, some in a landrover and in this way we visited remote lochs and linns in the Cairngorms too far to reach in an ordinary day's walking. Although the views from the top of the Allargue hill and from the march further up were among the most magnificent in Scotland remoteness always adds a measure of magic to a scene.

These longer distances demanded good shoeing and to begin with we went thirty miles down the road to the nearest forge suitable for horses, but when that blacksmith retired I decided to risk shoeing cold and the local smith came up and took measurements. It was very successful except that he never sent an account. Every time I passed him digging in his garden I said, 'Jimmy, could I please have a bill.' 'Yes, tonight,' he would reply, 'I'll sit down and make it out.' He was so convincing that I always believed him. After his death his widow sent in a bill for £16, which could only have represented a tiny proportion of the work he had done. It has always been a tradition of the glen for blacksmiths not to send bills. In the old laird's day

Family and friends with the ponies Rufus and Dorothy

the blacksmith in the Corgarff forge, closed half a century ago, sent in a bill for 12/6 for seven years work which included shoeing the Highland pony and many other things besides.

It seemed such a short time since Jimmy Massie had come to mend our cart and now we were going all over the county with the pony trailer to visit rallies and shows. He had warned me that my small estate van might split in two under the strain of pulling the trailer and one day it nearly did just that, causing me to pull into a garage, where the trailer was unhitched with the pony in it and a plate screwed on to the floor of the car. Ever since Seagull's arrival we had been showing at the local shows. At the beginning this was only in hand and at the first small show the only class was for roadsters, when a pony uglier than Dusty was pulled out and put first. Beneath me was an excellent local breeder of Highlands – a good lady whose father had been a railwayman and who had built up her business from nothing. 'I'm going out,' she whispered. 'Will you come?' Beneath her was a beautiful Welsh filly owned by a local laird. Out the three of us walked and I found the Secretary and told him what I thought of the judging. 'Fit's she blethering on about,' asked a man as I moved away. 'Aye,' came the answer, 'she's blethering like hell, but she's damn well right.' We decided to go to the larger shows, where the judging was first class and where my only anxiety was whether in the ridden classes Seagull and later Rufus would behave themselves with Hugh cantering round the huge ring in the parade at the end.

About a year before Jimmy died he had to give up shoeing my ponies and another smith came from further away. It was his heart that was the trouble. One evening, when the New Forest was young, he suddenly dropped his foot and spun round gripping the fence. 'What's he done?' I asked aghast. 'It's nae the pony,' he gasped out and I saw his ears were blue. 'Jimmy, get in the car and I'll take you home,' I said, realising he was having a heart attack. He turned in amazement, 'And leave the pony with twa nails in his foot,' he said, staggered at such a suggestion. He was still gasping for breath. 'What else can we do?' I asked. 'What else can we do? I'll put in the others of course.' 'Well, let me,' I pleaded, 'You tell me what to do and I'll do it.' 'Na. Na. You'll nae dae it right.' He put in the nails having attacks after each one because of the effort and constriction of the heart. I had never before seen such dedication to duty. It was typical of the man and of the place.

7

Scholars

Hugh started school just before his fifth birthday. The year before Mrs Campbell, the former school mistress, had encouraged him to attend, but he was too young. 'What's this I hear,' Agnes asked, 'about your not enjoying school?' A long pause and then the diplomatic reply, 'I think Candy (referring to her cross-Corgi) is a very nice dog, don't you?' Now the right age, cap squarely on head, satchel on back, he stumped off up the path not looking back. 'I've been learning French today,' he said on return. He knew French was a foreign language learnt at school, but what of course he had been learning from his fellow pupils was Doric and he soon became fluent in this dialect, reciting Burns and R.L. Stevenson in the vernacular. Doric is classical in origin – the earthiness of north east Scots is disciplined by the elegance and correctness of the classics, which were once taught in all parish schools of the area. It was not unusual in the early nineteenth century to see a man following the plough in the north east of Scotland with a copy of Virgil in his pocket. Doric expresses in grammatical prose the emotions and thoughts of one of the oldest heritages in the Kingdom. Burns wrote in Lallans, a language so flexible that it produced the couthiest and most exquisitely lyrical poetry in Britain; Violet Jacobs and other less well known poets wrote in the language of the north east and the two dialects, Lallans and Doric, blend together in Scottish literature to the benefit of both.

The teaching in Corgarff School was traditional and of a high standard. Under Mrs McIntyre, the schoolmistress, it was almost impossible to match it in any infant or primary school further south – whether state or independent. There was no nonsense and the children were well grounded with a mixture of innovation and habit-forming repetition. When a new stage of arithmetic was taught they went on doing examples until it was indelibly impressed on their minds. Yet so much enthusiasm was engendered that Hugh asked me to set sums for his amusement in the evening. Reading was mainly taught by phonetics, the aim of which is to eliminate failure, and this was combined with recognition or look-and-say, which invites faster reading among abler scholars but inhibits slower readers on account of its reliance upon memory. In the parish schools of earlier centuries concentration was primarily upon reading. In Walter Scott's novel *The Heart of Midlothian* Jeannie Deans says, 'My father wad hae wanted mony a thing before I wanted that schuling'. In those days fees were charged according to the difficulty of the subject. Thus reading was the cheapest subject taught, followed by writing and then arithmetic. Standards were high and it is reported that General Wolfe of Quebec fame was coached in mathematics by a parish school dominie when he was stationed in Inverness as a young officer. Latin was the most expensive subject, available to all who wanted it at the age of eight, regardless of whether or not their parents were fee paying.

The Corgarff school day was organised without haste or anxiety in ways tested by time and tailored to present circumstances. One morning we slept in. I was profuse in my apologies. 'Quite all right,' said the retired husband of the schoolmistress, 'No special hours'. Nothing could have been further from the truth but his Highland courtesy demanded that he put me at my ease. In previous centuries hours were rigorous, lasting from sunrise to sunset in winter when daylight hours were short and from seven in the morning to six in the evening in summer, with children who learnt Latin attending even earlier. In those days children brought peats for the school fire and the boys – who are called 'loons' in the north east, while the girls are called 'quinies' – chopped the sticks. Now the boys stacked firewood in the shed and carried it to the wood stove in the school room. Until recently the scholars brought their own 'piece' for a mid-day meal, but now the twenty desks were pushed a little closer than regulations allowed to make room for a partitioned-off tiny kitchen, where the postmistress' sister cooked a delicious hot lunch. The girls carried crockery and laid the tables, which tasks were performed at secondary schools in wartime Britain with no adverse effects on academic standards.

At the end of term there was prize giving at which each pupil received a prize on the principle that everyone can succeed at something. These extra prizes were bought with Mrs McIntyre's own money and the children sat round with shining faces waiting for their names to be called in a scene like one from Enid Blyton's book *Noddy Goes to School*. This enthusiastic involvement would have pleased the founder of Scottish state education, for John Knox believed that pupils should be equal and not excel against each other in 'sinful pride', while at the same time setting a standard of

Corgarth School c.1928: George Morrison 2nd from right, front row

excellence in which marks were added up at the end of the year – as was done in Corgarff – to produce a school dux. The schoolmistress had the gift of making all the pupils feel they mattered. If the two fostered out children – both well mannered and doing well – needed a hem turning or a button sewn on then out would come the needle and thread and their needs would be met. Following this example the children felt obliged to help each other and, as in other one-teacher Scottish schools, older children sat beside younger ones to help them with their work. Both parents and children knew that they had a teacher who upheld the finest traditions of the old school dominie.

What were these traditions and why was the parish school so important and influential? It has been truly said that, 'Elementary and secondary education met in that distinctly Scottish institution the parish school'. All children attended, thus forming friendships across the social divide. From earliest times it was possible for the poorest scholars to go from there straight to university. Although some students took no degrees and studied only chosen subjects nevertheless the ratio of graduates in the population was one in six, so that scholarship was widely diffused and, 'The intellectual aristocracy was much nearer the base than the apex of the social economic triangle'. Scottish universities, where the fees were astonishingly low but where the health of some students was permanently affected by their privations, were virtually class free, with every rank of society and income sharing the opportunities they provided. Although after the introduction of matriculation it was impossible to pass direct from these schools to university, nevertheless in 1940, when compulsory education still ended at fourteen, Nessie Templeton, the Allargue keeper's daughter, went straight from Corgarff School to secretarial college, where she won the highest award in Great Britain for typing and shorthand. Knox's vision had been to so educate the Scottish people that they would become literate and God fearing and he fitted into a democratic framework of kirk sessions, presbyteries, synods and Assembly the idea of national education for everyone. This was to be the first system of state education in Europe, with elementary, grammar and higher schools, as set out in his *Book of Discipline*. Able 'lads o' pairts' would go on to higher education, while less able scholars would be encouraged to study practical subjects, such as agriculture and navigation. Although lack of funds rendered these graded schools still-born at that time, nevertheless the aim of a school in every parish was steadily achieved within the next two centuries.

What were the origins of these traditions and how was this achievement brought about? As elsewhere in Europe the links between church and school went back to pre-Reformation antiquity. By the time the Celtic and Augustinian churches were absorbed into each other in the eleventh and twelfth centuries there were religious and educational foundations established in the north of Scotland at Dornoch, Fortrose, Inverness, Fearn, Kinloss and Beauly, from which Lord Lovat passed straight into Oxford University. Progress in education was, however, interrupted by the 300 Years' War with England, during which the Bishop of Moray awarded the first bursary for Scots students at Paris University, where a Scots College was opened in 1325. Then, after the founding of St Andrews, Glasgow and Aberdeen Universities in 1410, 1451 and 1494, James IV passed the first Education Act in the world in 1496 in order to provide a 'wise and learned judiciary'. Eldest sons of barons and freeholders were to attend schools from the age of eight and to remain at grammar schools until they 'be competently founded and have perfect Latin and thereafter remain three years at the schools of art and jure'.

Again, however, this dream was temporarily stultified by the English and French struggle for power in Scotland, leading to Flodden Field and the persecutions by Mary of Guise, the French-born Regent of Scotland, and consequent national and civil strife. This is why it fell to the exiled John Knox and to the Reformers to bring the dream of universal education to a poor and backward Scotland, with a baronage without the leisure for learning, few cities and a clergy out of all proportion in wealth and numbers to the rest of the population. The building of the schools and the schoolmasters' salaries were to be paid for by the lairds, who were not to be able to dismiss the dominie without fault and the new presbyteries were to see that schools were provided and inspected in every parish and that salaries were paid. By the time this was formally enacted at the end of the seventeenth century almost all the parishes of Aberdeenshire had schools. Subsequent improvements in agriculture enabled the tenants to contribute in kind, one bol of oatmeal for each plough in the parish. Parents were to pay fees but children whose parents could not afford them were to be paid for by the kirk sessions or educated free by dominies, whose own salaries were little above starvation level. In 1803 they were fixed until review at £16 a year, at a time when Robert Burns was drawing £50 for a minor excise duty.

In remote areas such as Corgarff the minister often acted as schoolmaster and differences in religion must sometimes have led to problems, particularly during the Covenanting period when the Marquis of Montrose used Corgarff Castle as a headquarters. Nevertheless, in Corgarff Parish School in the early nineteenth century Episcopalians, Roman Catholics and Presbyterians were reported to be learning the Presbyterian Catechism together, while elsewhere in the county inspectors noted a schoolmaster leaving out part of the text book on the Reformation because he had Roman Catholics in his school. At one time the dominie usually conducted the Sunday school on his one free day and, although the school teacher may not now be the Sunday school teacher also, nevertheless however empty the pews may be on the Sabbath, the Sunday school continues to flourish. This relationship between church and school, although less close than previously, remains alive today. 'What would you do?' an elderly minister asked the son of the Allargue keeper, 'if a man offered you strong drink?' 'Ask him to put water with it,' was the practical reply. The minister was a regular visitor when Hugh was at Corgarff School and most of the time that he was there he was fortunate in having a young minister who was a keen cricketer and waiting to become a naval chaplain. We took advantage of this by having the minister and the school to tea in the cottage followed by cricket coaching on the only flat field in the parish.

By the beginning of the nineteenth century the dream of a parish school in every parish in Scotland had nearly been attained. If there were shortcomings in the Highlands schools were paid for by The Scottish Society for the Propagation of Christian Knowledge (SPCK) and three Gaelic speaking organisations. In the north east in particular there was a deep reverence for learning, evidenced by the term 'scholar' being applied to every pupil and this tradition of excellence was given a boost in 1828 by the Dick Bequest, awarded to improve the standards of teaching in the area. Lengthy qualifying examinations, which graduates often failed once, entitled teachers to higher salaries fixed on a sliding scale – the more the lairds paid the more was added by the Dick Bequest. As in the Middle Ages boarded out scholars followed good teachers, who gave instruction free to less affluent pupils from far away. Latin was the most popular subject taught after reading and writing and in 1827 Greek was taught in all but two of the Aberdeenshire parish schools. It was said that it was the high standard of universal education that turned the northern Scots into the finest cattle breeders and stockmen in Britain. In the words of a contemporary French commentator, 'C'est les Georgiques a la main qu'on mieux laboure la terre'.

In the second half of the nineteenth century, however, Scottish urban education flourished at the expense of rural parish schools. Prior to the

1872 English Education Act, which brought compulsory elementary education to all citizens, and the Scottish Act of the same year, which offered grants to rural children proceeding to burgh schools, Parliament introduced a system of payment by results into Scottish education. This fixed grants on the number of pupils attending school and their proficiency in the three Rs and allowed no extra payment for complex subjects. The Scots objected on two counts; first, because the code did not allow for the teaching of classics and second, because it introduced class divisions into Scottish education by excluding the lairds' sons from eligibility for grant. Only on the second count were the Scots successful. On the first count no change was made for twenty-five years, when grants for specific subjects were at last increased in the Highlands and Islands – which area included Corgarff – but by that time rural education in Scotland had suffered and only in the counties receiving the Dick Bequest had standards been maintained.

Concurrently the Scottish principle of boarding out was accepted by Parliament, with a Committee recommending in 1888 that children in remote areas such as Corgarff should be boarded out if they wished to receive secondary education at a higher grade school. Because this was a Scottish tradition dating from the seventeenth century, when the Act of Icolmkill laid down that the men of the Isles should board out their sons on the mainland to receive a proper education, it had no detrimental effect on the parish schools, since it only drew off the outstanding 'lads of pairts' at a late stage in their education. Not so, however, the 1944 Education Act, which decreed that those who passed the eleven plus examination should be boarded out to attend the Senior Secondary School thirty miles away, while those who failed would travel daily to the new Junior Secondary School seventeen miles distant. During the long winter months bureaucracy placed these latter children's lives in danger, since regulations laid down that they must bicycle the last two miles home. Regardless of weather therefore they were picked up and dropped off at the junction, where the road south went off over the hills, and their bicycles were left all day in the ditch awaiting their return. If a storm blew up suddenly in Corgarff there was no way of contacting the driver and telling him to take the children back to Strathdon. Many representations were made over the years to councillors and MPs, but it was not until I discovered from a university acquaintance employed within the local department of education that it was legitimate for parents to ask for shelter that the matter was put right, after which the children were collected from and returned to the safety of Corgarff School.

The year after Hugh left the Parish School I was asked to fill a teaching gap in this Junior Secondary School. 'There she goes, fleein' doon the road,' said John Reid, the ex-postie, 'she'll be in hell or Towie in twenty minutes.' In fact I never did the journey in under twenty five. I found that the pupils attitude towards their teacher was courteous and self-disciplined and equated favourably with private rather than state education in England. The English regard education as a means to an end whereas the Scots believe it is an end in itself, allowing the participant to derive more pleasure and fulfilment from life and to hold his or her own in any environment. The teacher I replaced was responsible for time-keeping and bell ringing duties. The older boys did not want to see me over-burdened by extra curriculum activities in this way and offered to take over these duties themselves carrying them out with the greatest efficiency. Although education in basic subjects was good I met for the first time the phenomenon of pupils reading the Bible daily without any comprehension, a matter I had seen commented on in reports on Scottish education. The question, 'What have you just read?' brought the answer, 'I don't know.' Their compositions on the other hand were well expressed and grammatically correct and they said in one sentence what it would take an urban child to say in three. With wisdom the Scottish education authorities insist on pupils doing a fair copy of their corrected compositions and this sets a standard of excellence at which to aim in their next attempt. They used the vernacular freely within a disciplined grammatical syntax and I never suggested that they alter the words in any way. At first the boys and girls thought they might catch me out by talking broad Scots, but when this failed they reverted to their ordinary polite bilingualism, for all the people of the glens are broader in their speech when they are off duty than they are in the language they use in the professions or trades.

I was particularly struck by the standard of concentration, regardless of intellectual ability. Whereas a young person in an urban environment finds it difficult to sit still and needs periodic distractions, these young people found no difficulty in fixing their thoughts on a problem and keeping them fixed until the matter was resolved. On one occasion in a history lesson I saw Sandy Duncan, a Corgarff boy, staring at me with great intensity. 'Are you understanding what I am trying to explain?' I asked. 'Not all of it,' was the considered reply, 'but I'm understanding some of it and I am trying to understand the rest.' One girl was an eleven plus passer who had chosen not to be boarded out further down the road. She was the only pupil who put up her hand when I asked how many people formed visual pictures in their minds of stories that they were reading. This is of course the first sign of creative imagination, and it is to be feared that it could be inhibited by too much exposure to television and computers. All in all it was a happy school which excellently served the needs of these children, but with the introduction of comprehensive education it was closed and the children of the glen now travel thirty miles in each direction to attend what was the

A bad winter at Corgarff School

Senior Secondary School. The only way to obviate the strains of travelling this distance is to take the occasional day off and not push oneself too hard. Whether this is conducive to good scholarship must remain in doubt.

It was perhaps inevitable that when the schoolmistress retired the parish school itself would be in danger of closure. Knowing what was at stake the local newspaper released the story before the decision was taken. This was fortunate for in a bureaucracy once a decision is taken it is almost impossible to reverse it, the time given for later discussion being only a formality. The problem of course facing parents and educationalists alike was the snow in winter, which reaches fearsome proportions – both in the force of the wind and the amount of snow – in storms raging above 900 feet. This not only produces conditions of blind drift but deposits drifts of snow as high as twelve or fifteen feet. Perhaps for the children, however, a greater danger lay in the remarkable changeability of the weather among these hills. The wind whips up suddenly to gale force carrying armfuls of snow, and children could leave the village down the glen on a fine sunny afternoon and fail to get home at all. Journalists arrived in the village and the school hit the headlines in the national press as the 'School in the Clouds', articles stressing the courage of the inhabitants who were struggling to survive in a hostile environment. A meeting was called, a committee formed and a letter composed and sent to the authorities with copies to relevant people, both political and executive. An outstanding member of this committee was Dod Reid, a retired Allargue keeper, who demonstrated a remarkable aptitude for language. The letter drew immediate and concerned response. A further meeting was held by the local education officials, attended by elected representatives and civil servants. A tremendous turn-out of people filled the school to over-flowing. Speeches continued to drive home the point about the responsibility for the safety and lives of the children. The words expressed sincerely and eloquently went home. The unique situation of the village was appreciated and the school saved. Had it not been no families with children of primary school age would have come to the area, and the long process of death by depopulation would have been accelerated.

8

Winter

One glorious autumn I decided I would stay in the cottage throughout the coming winter. Agnes said nothing, but after lunch suggested taking the dogs for a walk. 'That's where the hares eat in the winter,' she observed, pointing to a ring round a tree about eight feet from the ground. I took the point, shut the cottage as usual and departed before the storms began.

What is it that is so compelling about these winter storms? It is the strength and bitterness of the wind, the wetness of the snow and the lack of visibility that combine to make unique conditions. A farmer, unable to see because of blind drift, can walk round and round in circles in deep snow in his own field until he is in a state of collapse. 'Robbie was nearly lost like that,' recounts his wife, who was amazed on that occasion to see a snowman stagger exhausted through the door and fall into his chair by the fire, when she thought he was in the byre minding the beasts. 'But the local people will survive where my men would have died', said a retired colonel of the 52nd Mountain Division, whose men trained in these hills in the war and whom I met years afterwards. I remembered his soldiers when they came to Allargue in 1942, their mules tethered to the fence behind the house. 'A fit man carrying routine equipment can only walk through soft snow to his thighs for less than a hundred yards before perishing,' the colonel continued, 'and the advantage that the local people have is that they understand and expect the conditions. Snow to them is an enemy but it is also an old friend. They know not to give it any chances, but they know how to get on with it if they are in trouble. Never fight cold, for it keeps the blood from the extremities anyway and if you go tense this process will be re-doubled and the extremities will be starved of vital supplies. They know that in all situations the snow is too wet and too soft to build into a snow house. The desire therefore to stop and rest on the snow is a choice which will bring death.'

This is a lesson that was again brought home to the glen when the doctor nearly lost his life going to a confinement up a long and exposed farm road.

He had told me on our arrival how on his way to visit our predecessors in the cottage in a bad storm, using his ski stick to test the way in front, the snow had suddenly risen up in his face in a violent upheaval. A sheep was buried under a drift and he had pierced its back, startling it out of a deathly slumber and in all probability saving its life. Fifteen years later, during a wild storm, Dr Reid answered a young husband's emergency call that his wife was in labour and he owed his survival on that occasion to Donald Gordon, a Strathdon keeper, who he had taken with him as well as the district nurse. The delivery successfully past the nurse remained with the new born baby and the two men set off for home. The snow was deep and the wind ferocious, carrying wet snow before it, driving it on to their faces and forming a mask through which it was almost impossible to breathe. The strength of the wind, the coldness of the air and the depth of the snow were exacerbated by the cloying dampness of the flakes. Sometimes in these conditions a scarf tied round the face preserves a pocket of warm breathable air; at other times it is necessary also to walk backwards and shelter the air with the body before it can be safely taken into the lungs. Meanwhile, despite protective clothing, the cold makes it difficult to preserve enough body warmth to counter hypothermia. Twice the doctor said that he could go no further. Twice he fell and asked to be left to lie down in the snow. 'Get up and keep moving,' the keeper said, propelling him through the drifts until they reached a house where he left him in the care of a kindly couple. By this time, however, his own judgement was impaired, for he had succumbed to that over-determination, almost like the 'bends', which is perhaps produced by the need to keep going or by the unrelenting whiteness of the surroundings or by the release of ozone into the air and this tempted him to test himself beyond the limit. 'I maun gang hame to feed the dogs,' he said, going out again into the storm. It was a decision that nearly cost him his life. Lost in blind drift he started going in circles. Then by a miracle he came to a fence where there were new posts and wire. He had mended it and knew where he was. Ten minutes later his wife saw the door suddenly flung open. Snow dropping everywhere he staggered across the room and fell on to the sofa. By the time she reached him he was asleep.

Blind drift is more dangerous than blizzards of fresh snow since it blows up in seconds without a cloud in a clear blue sky. The wind rises from nowhere, tearing up in its arms the top layers of snow, lashing them across hillsides with a force that blinds everyone in its path. Hence its name – blind or blin' drift. Whole masses of snow are removed from one hillside and deposited on another in a matter of moments. Hugh and I were nearly caught out in this way. One minute on a lovely sunny afternoon I was skiing at the bottom of the one-in-five main hill road while Hugh, aged eight, who was not long out of hospital after an operation, was snowballing with his anorak off, so enjoyable was the warmth of the sun. 'What a lovely afternoon,' I said to the passing shepherd. 'It a' depends fit ye're daein',' he replied without turning his head. Half an hour later Agnes passed on her way home. 'I think we had better go home soon', I said. 'If you don't go soon you won't get,' was her reply. It took a minute or two for me to realise that she was giving us a warning. The sky remained clear and the sunshine warm, but a wind was starting to rise. Immediately we set off for home and had we taken her route across the field, where there was less drifting all might have been well, but we went back the way we came, up the road, which the plough had not cleared. At the steepest part of the hill, where the drive turns in to Allargue House and the drifts were deepest, driving snowflakes borne on a whiplash wind took our breath away. 'I can't go any further,' said Hugh, the suddenness of his statement and the finality in the tone of his voice leaving me disconcerted and fearful. Mercifully we had an alternative – we could go back to the keeper's house on the other side of the road, warm ourselves by the fire and then with the aid of helping hands lift Hugh over the fences, back and forth, as the depth of snow varied between field and drive.

It is not until one has experienced it oneself that one fully understands how deceptive the weather can be in these high hills. The moment a blizzard or blind drift is past and the sun is out the beauty is bewitching. Everything is sparkling white except the sky, with the black line of walls or fences almost submerged and only the farmhouses and steadings standing out like blobs of paint. It is a friendly scene, but when the sunlight fades the unremitting whiteness of the snow, cast now in dark shadow, gives to the mountains and valleys a sense of eerie loneliness. It is the same lonesome feeling as that engendered by the sound of muffled snow falling upon roof or window panes, building up deep drifts against the house. When I was renovating the cottage, on one wild evening after darkness had fallen, the newly married wife of a farmer, who lived out-bye, wrapped her tiny baby in her shawl and set out through the snow to walk the mile to the hotel because her husband was working away from home and the loneliness of the storm had affected her nerves. She preferred to risk the wind and cold rather than remain alone through the night, knowing the depth of drift which could have built up against the outside door, necessitating the digging of a tunnel to open it. More usually, with the wind in the north, it is the back of the house that is affected. Once the laird made history by skiing up a huge drift behind the keeper's house and sailing over the front door in a magnificent ski jump. Until local people have known an incomer for many years they adopt a pose and minimise the unfavourable conditions. 'You should see it in a real January storm,' they say. Then one day you are one of them and their defences are down. 'It's starvation,' says postie as he steps over the threshold out of the wind. Perhaps it is because they fear weakening their own resolve that they do not dwell upon the dangers of the storms. Instead they taunt each other if the weather is rough in order that they are not tempted to remain by the fireside when there is outside work to be done. 'You're nae calt,' taunts the over-weight wife of a farmer, who is prevaricating about going out to sort the sheep. 'My bones are nearer the elements than yours,' he retorts good naturedly and the barb goes home.

Before there were ski lifts at the top of the hill, the glen was shut off from the north for weeks on end and the road over the hill was never opened until a storm was past. In radio broadcasts the road between Corgarff and Tomintoul was always the first to be closed. Even on the main road further down the glen the snow plough was routinely brought to a halt by drifts level with its roof and it had then to be dug out by men with shovels. A sign at the bottom of the hill would say the road was impassable but, the round trip being seventy miles, some motorists carried on until they stuck in a drift near the top and were then faced with staying in their car until the storm was past, hoping it would not be buried, or risking exposure and exhaustion in the two mile downward trek. One man spent two lonely nights in his car, while a blizzard raged preventing any rescue, but was guided down the third day, just before his car disappeared under a drift, by Geordie Cheyne, the Allargue keeper, who had heard of his plight from the police. The only food he had with him in the car were three jelly babies. Knowledge of the conditions removes any foolhardy temptation to move during a blizzard at that height but only detailed knowledge of terrain and wind reveals where the snow lies thinnest and where the deepest drifts settle. Over the latter skis and snow shoes are the only safe method of travel. In these bad storms no one ever needs to ask, 'Who is my neighbour?' Mrs Campbell, who was in charge of the school when we first came to the cottage, told me of her gratitude to my cousin Agnes, when her tiny baby was losing weight and her husband was away at the war. One night after it was dark and snow was falling there was a knock at the door of the shepherd's house in which she was living and opening it she found Agnes, clapping her skis together to remove the snow, with heavy kitchen

Lady Forbes with the keeper and his wife at the entrance to the Allargue drive

scales strapped to her back. She had heard of the mother's worry and set out to reassure her.

In the minds of these valiant lone skiers who had no safety bindings there never seems to have been thoughts of an accident, although this may not have been the case for those waiting at home. In those days parties would make long expeditions into the heart of the Cairngorms, climbing Ben Avon and staying over-night in a bothy more than twenty miles from medical help. All their skiing was in deep snow. They climbed with skins attached to their skis or by traversing back and forth upon the incline, with frequent kick turns. On the downward slope they turned by means of the graceful tellemark, predecessor to the snow plough and stem christie.

Now piste skiing has almost entirely superseded these far off past-times and the Cairngorm complex at Aviemore, leading with a chairlift right up into the mountains offers runs comparable to any on the continent in steepness and breadth, although, as in Norway, the unpredictability of the weather remains a problem. 'I've never seen anything like it,' one of the world's most experienced mountaineers was quoted in the press as saying, as he launched himself from the top of the White Lady chairlift into a combination of thick mist and howling gale. But see it on a sunny day in April and the view from the sheiling and the ski slopes is panoramic, equalled, but not surpassed by any in the world. One stands at the top of this high glen down which winds a burn and newly constructed road, looking towards the blue stretches of Loch Morlich, with its encircling band of dark fir trees, like a sapphire set among emeralds. Everywhere the mountains roll up and round to form protective shoulders and arms. It is in fact from such a spot that the vision of the Cairngorm complex was born in the mind of a young naval officer in the Second World War, who saw in a dream white sails on Loch Morlich. The feeling of warmth, camaraderie and internationalism that radiates the sheiling at the bottom of the chairlift is the same as that which lights the cafes at continental resorts. Even the children are present to form the familiar background, whizzing down the slopes with no fear and no sticks, singing and shouting as they go. But here, perhaps on account of the Scots' cheerful sense of inferiority for what they have to offer, there is less evidence of bad manners and over-competitiveness. On the days I have been at Aviemore no one has crashed

Digging out the snowplough at the summit of the Lecht
during 'the worst storm of the winter'

through a beginners' class, knocking everyone to right and left in a cascade of flailing arms, legs and sticks. No one has shouted *Achtung* from the top of a hill and plunged to the bottom, imagining that this magic word gives right of way through any crowd at any peril. Perhaps this teaching of skiing manners may go some way towards building up good Scottish resorts in defiance of that howling wind, which some maddening genie diverted to our shores.

Watching the Scots tackling the problems of wind, erratic snow conditions, blocked roads and poverty it is impossible not to be impressed by their courage, determination and toughness. At the top of the glen post-war skiing was for many years the 'climb up, ski down' variety of pre-war days. Then a tractor rope tow arrived, which was effective, provided one let go of the rope in sufficient time to avoid being pulled into the machinery. Later it was superseded by a short anchor tow, which, like the tractor, could be quickly moved if blind drift blew the snow from one hillside to another. More dangerous was a method of going up hill by parachutes which the skiers brought with them. These were of all colours, blue, orange and red and added to the already picturesque landscape. The wind billowed the parachutes out and the skier did not become airborne because a hole was pierced at the top. This was an upward journey requiring great skill, for the skier had to know which rope to release quickly to avoid being pulled over heather and rocks. No doubt it was on account of these very obvious dangers that, when the ski company was formed, with the road opened regularly to the better snow at the top, and longer anchor tows arrived, which had to be permanently fixed because of the weight of more people ascending, the parachutes and tractors were abandoned and the more traditional joys of piste skiing settled down to become the norm.

Ten years after we had left the cottage Hugh was waiting his turn in a queue for the ski lift. 'Have you skied here before?' he was asked. 'Yes,' he replied, 'I suppose you could say I christened the place by breaking my leg on this very slope before there were any lifts.' The problem then was the lack of facilities for mountain rescue and Hugh, who was fourteen, had broken his leg with a complicated spiral fracture. Friends had come to stay with us in order to ski and, although it was a little windy, it seemed a pity not to test the snow, which turned out to be sticky. I had stayed behind initially to finish making beds and followed the others up in my car. When I reached the bottom of the slope I saw a figure fall and not get up. It was Hugh. His safety bindings inexplicably had failed to open. When I climbed to him I saw his foot was hanging at a crazy angle. To remove the ski was agony but there was no alternative. It was not possible to complete the operation from below and I found it difficult to prevent myself sliding down the slope if I worked from above. To touch the leg at all added terribly to the pain. Mercifully we were a party of six that day, three adults and three young people. The mother of the two girls left to telephone for the doctor and ambulance, based in the village ten miles away. Agnes, who had joined us, put her arms under Hugh's back to lift him off the snow, for the wind was bitter and the snow wet. She pushed our anoraks beneath him in an effort to keep him dry. Down the slope I spotted a small ladder which had been used to make a ski jump, a welcome miracle, for we could use it as a stretcher. While one of the girls skied down to fetch it, I tied Hugh's ski against the outside of his leg as a splint. All this time he was heroic and uncomplaining.

In the distance on the road I was aware of a car stopping and the next moment a man arrived in his stockinged feet carrying a climbing rope. He provided the second miracle, the rope the third. With true British modesty he did not tell us then that he was a Royal Marine Commando trained in mountain rescue. I should have suspected such credentials on account of his stockinged feet, which I later realised prevented unwanted slipping, and his expert knowledge. For the moment therefore I continued giving instructions, relinquishing the job at once when I realised he knew all the knots with which to rope my son to the ladder. By now I had dug out a level platform below the place where Hugh lay on which we could put the ladder, so that the task of easing him on to it could be performed with least pain. His courage was remarkable and there were still no complaints. With the ski now splinted to his side we slipped him inch by inch on to the ladder and tied him on with the rope. Then we half pulled, half supported the ladder downhill over the snow, with his head first, for otherwise the leg would have pulled apart at the break. Once off the snow and on to the heather we lifted the ladder and started the long walk to the car from which we were separated by peat hags. The jolting, however, was intolerable and Hugh said, 'Stop!' By this time he had reached such a state of shock and cold that his teeth were chattering continually. We shed more clothes to cover him and mercifully at that moment the ambulance arrived. The doctor undid the splint, picked up Hugh's foot saying, 'This will hurt,' and jammed it back on to the limb, fixing a proper splint to it. It was an extraordinarily accurate set and had we taken him home instead of to the hospital the leg might even have mended satisfactorily, although of course it would have needed plaster.

An injection of morphia stopped Hugh's teeth from chattering. He was slipped from the ladder on to the stretcher and we carried him over the heather and peat hags to the ambulance. The injection made him talkative and he wanted to play word games all the way to hospital which we reached two hours later at 7 p.m., our friends and relations following in their own car and mine. By this time I was beginning to feel the strain myself and the kindness and concern of the ambulance man, who stayed with us to push the trolley when Hugh was admitted to a ward at 10 p.m. is a memory I shall never forget. We left him sitting up in bed reading *The Field* waiting to go to theatre for his leg to be set and I was told that visiting hours were strict and would not be until the following evening. Agnes went home in the ambulance and I went to stay with our friends. Healing was complicated, but two years later John was back on the slopes in Switzerland and fifteen years later was skiing again at the head of the glen.

The lifts, the chalet and the facilities for rescue have transformed the whole scene at the head of the glen during the winter. Where before there was silence, now when the snow is good there are buses and cars and skiers in their hundreds. The ski shop and restaurant are full of people hiring skis and boots and drinking and eating. Years before the editor of one of the magazines for which I had written an article on depopulation asked me to change the end to make it more cheerful. Although I appreciated the need to hold the reader's attention in this way, I could not think of anything to alter the unrelieved gloom engendered by the flight of people from the glens. At last, however, I had a breakthrough and wrote these words, 'But one day perhaps the glens will re-echo with voices, already there are signs of ski tracks in the snow'. Mercifully my words have come true to alleviate what was then the loneliness of winter and the skiers are bringing activity and a new dimension to the life of the area. But one wonders, as one watches them dashing past in cars between their houses and the head of the glen, whether they ever spare a thought for the people and the infrastructure that have made their sport possible.

9

The Hill

The Cairngorms, in the foothills of which the village of Corgarff lies, are claimed to be the only truly primeval areas left in Britain. The higher one climbs the more primeval do the flora and fauna become. The folds in the earth were thrown up during the volcanic period, crumpled, legend claims, in the fists of a giant or by the heaving of his shoulders against the floor of the earth. The remoteness and silence of the mountains and lochs within this natural stronghold impose a feeling of awe. Mountains rise to above 4,000 feet, dominating the wild ancient passes which generations have trod, disciplined by the fierceness of nature's forces. Ptarmigan live above 3,000 feet and in the surrounding foothills are grouse, black cock, grey hen and capercaillie. There are also snipe among the river bogs and 'blue' or mountain hares, which, like the ptarmigan, change their apparel to white in the winter to camouflage themselves among the snow. Lastly there are herds of shy red deer, commanded by antlered stags, the monarchs of the glens, which dwell on the higher slopes, coming down in winter and spring in search of food, and the gentle roe, which prefer the agricultural uplands and do not fear the human environment with the same primitive intensity. If all these species are protected from poaching and vermin and the numbers of one group are not allowed to advance at the expense of another, the animals and birds provide plentiful provender in the open season and enhance the economy of an area which would otherwise be barren.

The economy of the Highlands and upland northern areas of Scotland has traditionally been built on the cornerstones of grouse shooting and deer stalking, salmon and trout fishing, agriculture and forestry. Skiing, pony trekking and hill walking now also make a significant contribution to the tourist industry. Of these contributors grouse are the most exclusive in that they do not mix happily with the other parts of the economy. Their alliance with the sheep, from whom they took over after 1830 – when shooting rents began – as the greatest provider of wealth and employment in the glens, has not been entirely easy, in the sense that their different feeding requirements demand opposing heather burning policies. Unlike the sheep, which enjoy young heather shoots and in winter can scrape the snow away to clear them, grouse require plentiful supplies of longer older heather which provides them with nesting cover and winter food. Although arguments arise as to the benefits of grain to grouse, the amount of oats found in their crops in the old days of upland farming was proof of the contribution it made to their diet. Now, as agricultural technology advances, so have the stooks of oats on which they gorged in autumn disappeared from the landscape and been replaced by permanent pasture and woods. Grouse will not frequent the latter once young trees are up, nor will they fly over them, for the density of the forests acts as a magnet for vermin and provides impregnable cover for predators, so that the presence of a wood behind a line of butts or anywhere along a drive will turn grouse in ways that are not wanted. Moreover, experience seems to show that if the herds of deer increase the grouse decrease in inverse proportion. Deer – like cattle – tear heather up by the roots, reducing food supplies. Also the acute type of grouse disease, inflammation of the brain – the equivalent of louping ill in sheep – is carried by a tick on deer, which cannot be vaccinated against infection.

The reasons for periodic decreases in grouse population, the most recent, serious and dramatic being in the last six years, have defied all inquiries, but none has been as instructive, detailed, elegantly written or produced greater artistry than that published by the Board of Agriculture's Commission, 1905–11, entitled *The Grouse in Health and Disease,* on which Edward Wilson of the Antarctic served as field naturalist, physiologist, anatomist, part-writer and illustrator. After painstaking work Wilson traced the lingering form of grouse disease to minute threadworms (the strongyle) which crawl into the dew drops at the top of heather fronds and enter the bird's coeca, affecting its membranes, particularly if it is weak or starving. Wilson listed a healthy bird's diet as heather (particularly green shoots and at the dwarf heather stage), berries (cran, crow and blae), heads of rushes, bog myrtle buds, seeds, insects (recently in short supply) and oats. He noted that wet sour husks are not ideal food, but nevertheless 'when the oats have ripened well the stock of grouse the following spring is healthy and vigorous and the breeding season is a good one'. He summarised reasons for mortality as: accidents (such as flying into wires), extremes of climate, predators, exigencies of reproduction, exhaustion, deficiencies of diet, grit or water (grouse do drink so artificial water courses are essential in a dry season), excessive heather burning, wet hatching seasons, frost and wind killing heather, and deep snow with frost preventing feeding through hard crust. Although Wilson did not advocate wholesale destruction of vermin it is impossible to believe that he would have approved the importation or artificial breeding of birds of prey or misguided current legislation – The Wildlife and Countryside Act 1981 and the application of the EC Wild Birds Directive – that prevents keepers destroying or even frightening birds of prey known to be killing grouse. Lord Lovat in the same report catalogued these birds and animals as: foxes, stoats, weasels, peregrines (which kill grouse in flight), hooded crows (a pair nesting in a plantation can eat 100 grouse eggs), rooks, jackdaws, ravens, golden eagles (too impressive to be called vermin), and hawks – of these latter, kestrels kill rats and mice as well as grouse, while hen harriers prey on grouse and buzzards confine themselves to smaller birds, including grouse chicks. Predators on the wing can cause grouse to flee in terror and if panic precludes a peaceful life the birds migrate to safer places, leaving the economy of an area ruined, with many people out of a job. It is not only grouse that are affected by the protection of these predators, but smaller birds also, which are fast disappearing from the gardens and fields.

The protection and nurture of grouse is a task for all seasons prior to 12 August (The Glorious Twelfth), laid down in 1773 as the start of the open season, and activity on the hill never ceases except when deep snow is on the ground, when breaking the frozen crust is the only task possible. Moors and areas vie with one another on that day, not only as to the number of birds seen and shot, but as to the proportion of old to young birds, the latter of which form next year's stock. A moor should be left in the autumn with the number of grouse it will support in winter and early spring and the purpose of good shooting is to ensure that this is done and, by avoiding over-shooting, to leave enough young birds to maintain a healthy stock. Preparations will have been arduous, starting with the burning of old heather, the keeping down of vermin, ensuring as far as possible food and water supplies and preparing the butts for the guns. Everything in this programme depends on a good keeper's conscience, for only this will drive him from his fireside out to a fox's lair at night or to a distant chilly spot to sit and wait for a hoody crow. To those who feel that a gamekeeper's work is a heartless task geared to the annual culling of his stock, one can reply that there is no difference between this aim and that of a farmer feeding store cattle to provide meat for the table. Whereas beef or 'butcher meat' as it is called in north east Scotland is closely identified with English life, the Highland Scots have always eaten more of the crops of their land – sheep, grouse, venison, pigeon, hare, salmon, trout, or, prior to the disease of myxomatosis, the humble rabbit.

In the glen, smoke from March fires heralds the start of spring when the old heather is burnt to encourage young shoots. Fire stimulates growth from the roots, but if the heather is old and long the heat germinates seed lying under the soil. Balanced burning in patches and long strips – thirty to forty yards wide – produces plentiful supplies of all stages of heather and a 25-year rotation means that seven times the number of grouse can be carried than would be the case with a 100-year rotation. Young sprigs graduate after five years to become springy medium sized heather for another ten years before moving up again for a further ten to remain in their natural state, with long woody stem and flower so far from the root that growth is inhibited. Grouse are renowned family lovers and once they have secured their own territory and found a mate they appreciate strip farming just as did the ancient Britons. Therefore tufts should be left for nests, bare ground for sunbathing, older heather for seed, shelter and concealment, young heather for food and burnt clear patches in favourite spots, such as by burns or on sunny knolls. Occasional scattered areas of grass produce grazing for sheep, whose droppings attract insects. Local experiments have shown that where the heather has been torn up and the area re-seeded with grass the heather does not return even at 1,500 feet and higher, and thus it is open to

Heather burning on Allargue

question how much grass grew in these hills 200 years ago when cattle still fed upon them in summer. Insects also inhabit the bogs, home of the cotton grass flower, which is a favourite tit-bit for both grouse and sheep.

If a fire gets away from a keeper it puts the rotation of the moor out of balance and is a disaster for the grouse, but a plus for the sheep. A single keeper burning alone is therefore a hazard to himself and the moor, but if he is fit and has a good strong heart and lungs he can just manage. The secret of success is to be sure that the broom handled wire netting beater has really knocked the heart out of one section of smouldering fire before abandoning it as dead and setting off up or down the hill to control another section. It is the running back and forth up and down to cope with renewed fires breaking out again which is the killer, together with the heat of the fire and the exertion of beating, particularly if the weather is warm. There are various tactics which a keeper burning on his own or with limited help can put into practice. Although old heather is best burnt against the lie of the sticks and fires lit against the wind give the cleanest burn, nevertheless fires can be started with or against the wind, or in the direction of water or a snow drift. There are also compensations in having few distractions. It is for instance an ideal time to test the obedience of a dog in training, for as the keeper goes from one fire to another a young dog can be told to sit and stay until he returns. I remember in the war a golden Labrador puppy at Allargue called Fay which Templeton the keeper carried home in the folds of his coat because the day and the fires were so hot that she was made tired by all the climbing.

Templeton was a remarkable man. He and his wife were both fine looking, as were their children – their eldest son wearing the beret of the Commandos. Lord Lovat in the 1911 Inquiry wrote that good keepers he had known had knowledge, powers of organisation, a sense of responsibility and were prepared for hard work. They were also articulate and shrewd, 'Men of few words in company but with power of expansion when the audience is congenial, eager to learn and accept new views and facts'. Had he been alive today he might also have added that they are law-abiding people whose jobs are in conflict with present legislation. Templeton's favourite sayings have survived his death, 'A yoking broken is a yoking lost' and 'Here's a thing I've never done before, but I'll fairly try it now'. As well as doing his job as keeper he also acted in the war as farm grieve. By the university summer vacation of 1944 I was eighteen and allowed to serve in the Observer Corps, but in April 1943 I was still only sixteen and work on the land was the only option open. It was also beneficial because I had affected my health by too much academic study. I therefore went north in that year for the spring and summer vacations to help in any way I could on the hill or on the farm. Since in both years – 1942 and 1943 – I shot in line with my father and brother for a fortnight in August I had two prejudices to overcome – in local language I was a 'toff and a quine' – but under Templeton's instruction I mastered the various tasks in which we were engaged. The First World War had made a deep impression on him. When we crossed the river in search of deer which were eating the green corn he would wade over in brogues and stockings saying, 'We're crossing the Marne'. He had mountaineer's eyes which looked beyond one into the distance. He always carried a crook and walked with a slow, steady, purposeful rhythm that was easy to follow. On one occasion we were lost in a mist after a visit to a foxes' lair and I followed his boots up and down gullies until we came to a burn which I expected to be flowing in the opposite direction. My disorientation in that fog was something I never forgot. On a clear day Templeton would stop, spotting in the far distance a bird of prey, a deer or a fox, perhaps using his spy glass, one foot in front of the other, leaning on his crook. He identified with the place, arrived every morning for what he called his orders and worked as many hours as there were in the day.

The nesting season follows the burning and what the grouse want then is moderate weather and peace and quiet. Storms of snow and heavy drifting in very late April and early May will decimate the grouse for that year and ruin the breeding season. April is one of the busiest times in the keeper's calendar, for it is also the month of the foxes. I found, when I was living in the cottage, that Geordie Cheyne the keeper was involved in that month in round-the-clock vigils on the hill. 'Ah weel, I'll be at the foxes the morn', is the answer you get when you need a helping hand, except for those few evenings when there is no plan to wait at a lair. Terriers are an essential part of the programme. Most keepers used to have cairns, the smaller wiry variety not shown at Crufts, which are capable of bravely taking on a fox to the death or of flushing it out at a place where the keeper is waiting with his gun. Jack Russells, which have always been used for foxes in hunting counties, riding in the huntsman's pocket if they are tired, are now becoming more popular in the north where they fit into a game bag if the heather gets too long for their short little legs. A foxes' lair is a cruel sight and a visit there an experience I have never forgotten. The fox kills for love of killing and scatters the half eaten prey around its home so that it is difficult to feel pity for him or his vixen. Dead hens, rabbits and other

Archie Templeton and his son David with panier ponies – 'guns' in the distance

defenceless animals are strewn around, a head torn off here and a leg there and the corpse is then abandoned as the fox turns its attention to the pleasure of hunting and killing another prey. Nevertheless the cubs are round and furry, despite fleas, and sometimes a survivor has been carried home in a keeper's bag to become a children's pet. One arrived thus at the

Allargue Hotel on a snowy night and was brought up with the dogs, sitting with them on a couch looking at television until he grew up and killed chickens. A home was then found for him at an English zoo from which he escaped and, chased by men with guns, entered a house and sought sanctuary on a sofa in front of television. Returned to the zoo this story made front page news in the tabloid press.

On another occasion it was a baby red deer which became a pet at the home of the Allargue keeper and later when he was fully grown was transferred to a zoo. He had come with his mother in early spring in search of food and she had been shot. In those days Allargue was not a deer forest. Stags came in occasionally but the only dependable stalking was of hinds in November, which provided an income from venison. Now, as the population of red deer increases, so do stags come down regularly from the Cairngorms in the rutting season, but stalking only lasts two or three weeks before the close season begins. The keeper who succeeded Templeton claimed that he could persuade more beasts over the march by imitating the roaring of a rutting stag. During the war when oats were grown and every morsel of food was valuable and needed protection, stags with their antlers still in velvet led their herds down at night in June to feed and returned to the tops by day. Waiting in the evening for them to come in was a long drawn out affair, because it was often not until too dark to shoot that the stately line of beasts appeared on the skyline silhouetted against the darkening sky. The only tactic then was to go home and rise the following morning at 4 o'clock when, although it was broad daylight, the herd could not tear themselves away from the delicious feed. Shooting over the river from a neighbouring drive so as not to disturb the deer I wounded a stag, rendering it immobile. Nevertheless a young stag refused to leave his side and even tried to snuffle him back to life when – after we had forded the river and crawled behind a wall – Templeton finished off the old stag with a second shot. I persuaded the keeper against his better judgement to spare his young and noble companion's life and only when we had fired a third warning shot and appeared from behind the wall did he at last run off after the herd. 'I have never seen the like of that before', said Templeton. I have not shot a deer since that day and, while recognising the urgent need for others to do so, agree with my father, who said that it would be a splendid sport if you could take off your hat to the stag when you got within shot. Back at the game larder Xanthe, my youngest cousin, clad in summer dress and sunbonnet, had a more practical and less sentimental approach. Aged three and destined to become an able and sympathetic doctor, she wielded a little axe on the recumbent animal, repeating to herself at intervals, 'Poor 'tag, poor 'tag'.

As summer ripens and 12 August approaches butts have to be repaired for the grouse drives. Supported by stakes, earth and heather, sods are built into a camouflaged wall – low enough to rest the elbows upon while waiting for drives to come in – while the bottom of the butt is dug out to protect from sight a gun and sometimes a loader and marker, whose task it is to mark the place the birds have fallen so that they can be picked up after the drive. The position of the butts, half hidden under the hill, creates the character of the drive. Sometimes the skyline is so short – as with one famous drive at Allargue – that only those with the most accurate vision, quickest reaction, straightest eye and greatest precision of movement can bring down birds in front. Other butts have longer vision and rely for natural cover on the length of heather and contour of the slope. All are set straight across the natural line of flight in full view of each other. At last the day arrives when over the moors of Scotland and parts of England and Wales beaters with white flags line out across the hillsides. A whistle is blown by the leader and the first drive begins. The white flags of the beaters appearing round the side of a distant hill usually heralds the approach of the first birds. By late autumn they have become wilder and fly faster in packs, so that to shoot a right and left in front and behind becomes virtually impossible for all but the finest shots.

On Allargue it has been the practice for the laird to walk the hill with four or five guns in line until the whole hill has been covered which takes two weeks. Only after that does driving commence. This programme was followed and handed on by Agnes' father, Colonel David Wilson Farquharson, under whose care the moor became the finest of its size in Scotland. Walking in line, climbing up hills and down gullies, is one of the most interesting and enjoyable past-times and in a good season daily bags of well over a hundred brace have been achieved at minimum cost. The steady movement of the line across the heather puts the birds up at the right distance. Experts say the shots are similar – a bird on the wing going away – but the beauty of the scenery and the challenge of the difficult hill walking combined with the concentration necessary for accurate shooting are a splendid compensation. The rules are strict: never shoot down the line; don't get out of line by going too fast, which will put birds up too soon, or by falling behind, which means a shot cannot be taken at the back if a bird has lain too close; when the line swings out to turn like a cartwheel remember that the flank must walk faster than the centre; don't talk because the grouse will hear and get up out of shot; don't shoot too close – give the birds a chance to get up properly – and don't shoot cheepers.

Dogs and ponies have traditionally been part of the grouse shooting season and the training of dogs, retrievers and to a lesser extent pointers, is an important part of the preparation for the 12th. Sometimes at Allargue pointers were hired with their handlers, working the ground in pairs in front of the guns, scenting and pointing with their noses, one paw raised, at a sitting grouse. In the war Templeton trained a golden Labrador Twink to perform both functions – pointing and retrieving – but she did not hand on this rare quality to her daughter Fay and the strain died out. Sometimes a dog retrieves a grouse so fast that the guns barely halt, at other times the dog is slow and scent unreliable and the walking line enjoys a welcome pause. A well trained dog with a good nose makes its owner a popular man – in the old days a less obedient dog, his presence justified by a good nose, would strain at a leash in the hands of a stalwart walking in line with a game bag, for no gun then attached a dog to his belt. Carriers were then less laden, for good organisation meant that piles of grouse could be left at intervals for the panier pony coming behind, but now mechanisation has replaced the pony with an 'argo cat' which cannot penetrate boggy land. The pony man was an expert. His pace was slow but his route required great expertise and knowledge of the hill because of the undetectable Highland bogs to which his heavily laden pony was vulnerable and from which, once in, it was difficult to be extracted.

Coming in one day from shooting in line at Allargue in the late 1940s after a lucky afternoon, another guest said to me, 'You may be only a woman but you're a damn good shot'. His remark emphasised that shooting is a man's sport and although I had enjoyed it I decided to concentrate on other sports that I enjoyed equally and leave shooting to the men. My training, however, enabled me, after we had moved into the cottage, to help Hugh with his shooting and he not only enjoyed boys' shoots at Allargue but also received valuable instruction from the keeper. Moreover he was able as a teenager to go beating on Allargue and neighbouring moors which was a good source of income in the holidays. Beating is now not as arduous as once it was because teams are convoyed outwards in landrovers. Motor cars also enable them to come from far and wide and a natural reserve brings a companionship of silence which older local members share with each other as they all drive out to the starting point.

Meanwhile guns, loaders, markers, and flankers – be they guests or keepers – walk or drive out to the butts together, dressed in tweeds, with

Labradors and spaniels running at their heels. Sometimes keepers will act as loaders but usually they are out on the flanks trying to prevent the birds from breaking out above or below the butts. The task requires concentration and quickness of reaction, for if a flanker rises too quickly from the heather he will send the grouse back over the beaters, but if he waits too long the speed at which the grouse are coming means they cannot be turned. There is just one moment when the flanker must leap to his feet and wave his white flag for all his worth. I only shot once from a butt with no success, but I prided myself on the standard of my flanking which I much enjoyed. On one occasion an over zealous gun sent a rain of shot dropping from the sky on to the heather around us, and then the sport became a little too exciting, for as soon as our flags were waved we had to fall into the heather to protect ourselves from the scatter. On another occasion I came back over the hill in my car and met the guns. 'Come and join us,' everyone said. 'What would you like to do? Will you act as marker in a butt or will you flank?' 'I could do with another flanker,' said the keeper hopefully. 'But I haven't got a flag,' I replied. Then I remembered that before I went out to luncheon I had collected the laundry. Complete with pillow case attached to a borrowed stick I joined the party. This is all part of the way of life in the glens and it is impossible to contemplate the desolation, unemployment and economic ruin that will face everyone if this time the grouse have truly gone never to return – fleeing from the uncontrolled killing of the protected predators.

10

Agriculture, Forestry and Fishing

Since the beginning of the last century no one has solved the problems of the Highland economy. That was the time when the boom in black cattle grazing the upland grass ended and the sheep arrived in large numbers, bringing smaller profits and souring the land. Poor harvests had affected the downland farms towards the end of the eighteenth century and the sheep in those farms were in a parlous condition with few shepherds, so that the opportunities offered by empty wastelands in the Highlands came just in time. In the following 150 years the population of the glen halved, due to voluntary not imposed emigration. Here the sheep were owned by tenant farmers and travelling shepherds and not, as in some Highland areas, by the landlords. Slowly the numbers of sheep versus cattle in the wider strath multiplied, from 4 to 1 in 1800 to 11 to 1 in 1960. In the Highlands it seems that everything landowners tried to do to make their estates viable and keep the people on the land failed. Undoubtedly some lairds wished to increase or maintain their wealth at the expense of their tenants, but J.G. Lockhart recounts in his life of Sir Walter Scott how the laird of Staffa achieved the ambitious target of doubling the numbers of people residing happily on his land and trebling his income. Yet, as Lockhart writes, 'Changes in public policy within a few years destroyed the ease and prosperity' which Scott had witnessed. Failure to stop emigration took place despite the efforts of philanthropic landlords, who, in the nineteenth century, perhaps particularly in the north east, built and helped to maintain schools, churches, manses, village halls, bridges, farmhouses and steadings, contributing to the salary of the schoolmaster and stipend of the minister and spending more money than they could afford on the welfare of their tenants. 'The purse of such men was open for every good cause,' wrote a renowned citizen of India of the laird's great great grandfather, who spent his early adult life in the sub continent. 'They showed,' he said, 'commercial integrity and liberality, active kindness and unwearied charity.'

The poverty of the Highlands and upland areas of northern Scotland at the time of Union in 1707 was of a scale unknown in Great Britain. The economy revolved round the breed of small black cattle, which thrived on the good quality upland grass along the rivers and among the heather, and after the Union the beasts were driven south for sale in the autumn, leaving the breeding stock wintering down country or in the byres. Because of the extensive hill grazing to which they had access, the people of Corgarff ran more cattle than their brethren further down the strath and were thus more punctual in their payment of rents, which in the second half of the eighteenth century doubled in some Highland areas and tripled in others, enabling them to remain static – even to the pound – for nearly half a century, from 1870 to the end of the First World War. In some of the glens surrounding the strath the moor grazing was held in common with numbers of stock broadly agreed, but in Corgarff an average hill holding of 500 acres per farm was scaled to the size of the arable unit. By 1843 the cattle were either sold in Aberdeen, where they made high prices and were then shipped to London, or sold to local or visiting drovers who took them to the trysts at Falkirk, being entrained at a later date from local railway stations. The Corgarff arable holdings, running from 30 to 150 acres, were sufficiently small to be run by families, requiring very few servants, and, although harvests were often ruined by frost, wind, rain and sometimes even snow, with two months probably passing between cutting the corn and leading it home, nevertheless rents were as high as in the wider strath on account of the valuable hill grazing. In the eighteenth century cattle were still used for ploughing near Aberdeen and at the start of the nineteenth century there were only fifty horse drawn carts in the strath, with dung still being carried to the fields in creels. In those parts of the Highlands where garrons ran wild on the hills, the people always used horses for ploughing but in Corgarff the steepness of the slopes demanded that four horses be yoked together, one man following the plough, another walking backwards at their heads to encourage greater effort.

There were in those days a variety of crops grown on the upland farms: bear – a type of four-rowed barley; oats – a quick ripening short oat was grown in Corgarff; turnips and potatoes. By mid-nineteenth century the infields, which were divided by stone dykes, carried a seven-year rotation of oats twice, turnips, bear, hay and two years' pasture, followed later in the century by a five-year rotation of oats, turnips, bear, hay and two years' pasture. The outfields were first divided into folds, where milking cows were regularly enclosed and moved to produce dung, and faughs which were rib ploughed and grazed or left barren. After that the outfields were sown with oats which produced the successive scanty crops upon which Sir Walter Scott commented in *Waverley*. The haughs, being marshy, were kept in permanent pasture. Hill grazings were marked by cairns and when the cattle and sheep were on the hill it is probable that, as in Scandinavia and Switzerland, they were herded by the family.

On the Allargue estate little townships of half a dozen houses clustered round the burns and roadways and these, together with the five outlying farms, made up the westernmost part of the self sufficient village of Corgarff. The people produced their own food, flailed, winnowed and later threshed their corn and milled their oatmeal, which, together with vegetables, dairy products, pigeons and rabbits was their staple diet. Meat was cooked with vegetables and barley in the soup pan which hung on a sway over the open fire. While the women spun wool, knitted socks and pullovers and weaved cloth, the men engaged in many trades, including joinery, tailoring, weaving, iron foundring and the making of spoons and other implements from horn. In Corgarff there was a reported shortage of shoemakers and masons. In all estates the tenants came twice a year to pay rent and present grievances ameliorated by the laird's whisky, and, if the chieftain or laird could afford a banquet, as described from eye witness accounts in Scott's *Waverley,* all tenants would be present, seated according to rank, while round the table marched the piper serenading the guests. The barbaric feuds which bedevil Scottish history were now on the wane and being replaced by courteous hospitality which was also a traditional way of life. French wines as well as whisky were available in many Highland public houses, but Corgarff remained renowned for its smuggling and illicit stills, fines for which were paid from a common fund. Improvements to buildings did not necessarily raise the rent by the expected four and a half per cent, since costs were shared between landlord and tenant, the laird supplying the materials and the tenants the labour. The heather-roofed houses of the eighteenth century with a hole in the ceiling to let out smoke from the fire were replaced in the nineteenth by slated farm steadings and houses lined with lathe and plaster. The fuel burnt was mainly peat, the cutting of which from a common hag was a right for all tenants, leading in one instant further down the strath to a bitter dispute that caused villagers to set fire to each other's fuel. Both these rights and the methods of cutting and drying have survived unchanged to the present day. An elongated spade with a ridge on one side cuts the peats, which are then set up in tripods for drying. Sometimes the ground, which is rich in minerals, provides one layer of peat, sometimes three or four. In the war, when I was staying at Allargue, the whole family went out on occasions to help the keeper cut, set up and bring in the winter peats. In the mid-nineteenth century an iron mine operated briefly on Allargue one mile short of the march on the northern route over the hills, while a slate quarry three miles further on provided slates for local roofs. There were also eight limestone quarries in the strath, which, with the aid of the tenants' own kilns, provided fertiliser for the stony soil, which required arduous trenching and draining.

By the Second World War many townships on Allargue were no more than heaps of stones along the roads and burns, while further west, running up the river, one farm was a ruin and three abandoned, with the land being grazed and cultivated by the home farm and those holdings still with tenants. Before and during the war the farmers owned no tractors of their own, they cut the corn with binders pulled by two horses and on some small holdings they still used the scythe. The tenants had, however, before the war formed an association which loaned out equipment – including one tractor – to its seventy members who paid for the hire. The task of clipping the thousands of sheep was entirely by hand. At least three times a year they were rounded up off the hill, twice for dipping and once for clipping, when they were brought down to the farm which provided the best pens. The farmers worked together at the clipping and there was great rivalry between them, with some individuals shearing as many as 200 sheep in one day.

In 1942 Agnes took over the running of the home farm herself after her husband had been sent to India and she moved her family and the inestimable Nanny into the hotel, which was no longer running commercially, but which stood on the main road at the bottom of the hill, so that it was more accessible to the snow plough. At the start of her farming career she employed and fed a young man who lived in the bothy and a landgirl who stayed in the hotel, but by the following June the farm was being worked by the keeper alone with any part time help that could be found. In that month the priority task was hoeing turnips and when I went to stay in my university vacation in order to help in any way I could I was constantly reminded of Templeton's saying, 'Here's a thing I've never tried before but I'll fairly try it now'. The turnips had already been ridged and one seedling every six inches had to be given room to swell by striking out the others with a deft movement of the hoe. We made up a team of four, working at the same rhythmic pace. In that year the start of the harvest coincided with the last days of walking up the grouse on the hill and in the late afternoon, or if it was raining hard and the shooting had to stop we stooked sheaves instead. In September I returned for the leading of the corn, home to the stacks behind the hotel, working with Templeton and the stalwart Prince who knew the task backwards and stopped at each stook without a word of command. One night, just as dusk fell the whole load 'couped' on to the roadside and the memory of the keeper's patience is as real today as it was then when in the gloaming we laboriously loaded the whole cart again from the bottom.

Archie Templeton with farm horses during the war

By the time I was back in the glen and renovating the cottage Agnes' sister Jean had moved into the nearest of the abandoned farm houses on the river as a summer residence, braving five gates enclosing stock and one and a half miles of rough track, and, following her lead, another family took the house beyond as a holiday cottage. Just months before our arrival the laird had retired from the army and was farming the home farm himself with the aid of a part-time grieve – who was also the hotelier – a shepherd and some casual labour. He believed in participating in all manual tasks and prided himself on the speed of his turnip hoeing. After setting the pace for most of the day he would put aside his hoe and set off to fish in the river leaving an exhausted team behind him to finish their hours of work. By now horse power was only a memory and, although a garron mare and two foals made up the stock complement, it was the tractor which towed the sheaves home to the stacks behind the hotel. The laird was, however, still expert with the scythe, scything grass beside the drive and house long past his eightieth birthday. He bred cattle and ran 500 breeding ewes, the latter of which he fed on home-grown turnips and oil seed rape. Some of the calves he sold in the autumn, others he kept to sell in the spring, wintering them with the cows in the byre, where they fed on threshed corn and hay. Without the marginal aid production and hill farming subsidies there would have been no profit and because he was running the farm with paid labour, there was almost always a small loss.

The marginal nature of these upland farms brought changes in the glen in the late fifties and early sixties, both as regards the extent of woodlands and security of tenure. In 1958 the Agriculture Act was passed with no special provisions for Scotland, under which landlords were given greater authority and freedom both to raise rents and give notice to quit. A tenant was no longer able to bequeath a lease if a landlord wished to take a farm into owner occupation upon his death. In England this reversed post-war legislation, but in Scotland, where land holding had a different tradition, it took the position back to the end of the last century. To understand why, it is necessary also to understand how the traditions of land holding between the two countries developed differently owing to the prolonging of the feudal or clan/family period in Scotland. Here, until the middle of the eighteenth century, there was less freeholding, but a very high degree of security of tenure for the tenant, despite the fact that Scottish leases were often not written down and consequently difficult to prove. Kings, nobles, chieftains and heads of families depended upon the supply of men for their armies of freebooting raiders, in return for which they provided protection and land. Thus holdings were never broken up into saleable parcels as happened in England after the earlier end of the feudal period, when lawyers devised ingenious schemes for breaking entails. In the Scottish Lowlands tenants had enjoyed security against purchasers since 1449 and could hand on leases from father to son in a system of 'kindly' tenancies, while in the Highlands, where the chieftain's relations were the middle or tacksmen, all land was held in perpetuity, provided no transgression was committed which brought the perpetrator before the chieftain's heritable court.

One year after the crushing of the 1745 Rebellion this system of land tenure was replaced by rent paid in money and kind and the chieftains were turned into landlords on the English model, owning larger estates than their southern equivalents and with their legal and heritable jurisdiction removed in return for compensation. This new lack of security for tenants, coming as it did just before a series of bad harvests in the second half of the eighteenth century led to such hardship throughout the whole farming community of Scotland that tenants could not be found. In 1770 therefore an Act was passed to encourage the life tenants of entailed estates to grant longer leases by making it legal to draw up a lease for thirty one years or the period of two lives. When this did not bring sufficient security to prevent continued dispossession and lack of good tenants coming forward, another Act was passed in 1883 – the Agricultural Holdings (Amendment) (Scotland) Act – which restored the ancient right of tenants to bequeath a lease to a chosen heir. This Act came three years after the rubicon of 1880 in which it was said that agriculture ceased to produce a profit. Mr Smith, MP, a member of the Gladstone government, commented that, 'Large tracts of the Highlands have been turned into wildernesses and it seems at this time almost too late to bring back the native population'.

Between 1958 – when this right to bequeath a lease was taken away – and 1968, when the right was restored for close relatives – endorsed again with modifications in 1983 – there were changes in agricultural holdings all over Scotland, as landlords understandably took advantage of an opportunity (which might not last) to raise rents or reclaim land. In some places, including the strath, the situation was complicated by the opportunities offered to tree planters who were allowed to postpone and stagger death duties to dates in the future. Two World Wars had decimated the tree capital of the country, forests were felled and not replanted and governments of both persuasions not only allowed trees to rank as a separate estate for taxation purposes, with tax not payable until felling or sale, but also offered generous planting grants to increase afforestation. These grants were not scaled to the difficulty of the land planted and thus agricultural land was attractive because it had been tilled and was already fenced, although not for rabbits or deer. As farms in the area came into hand and were planted up, resentment crept in where previously there had been goodwill. Improvements to and good maintenance of tenanted hill farms are not necessarily economic, but they bring gratitude in their wake.

The tenants argued from the point of view of agriculture, sociology and scenery. Their ancestors, they said, had wrested this land from nature, removed the rocks and tilled the soil and latterly they had received grants to do so. Now a tradition of tenant farming was being substantially eroded, while up and down the strath, scenes of beauty in the valley and by the river were being overwhelmed by conifers. The landlord, however, was more induced by financial considerations, for including subsidies a man farming 100 acres of arable land and 500 hill could not make a profit of more than £10 an arable acre in the currency value of the day, and on a smaller farm the figure would be nearer £7. Rents in the area were £3 an acre and if they had gone up significantly (and they did not do so in the relevant ten year period) tenants would have been unable to pay. Profits on the other hand from trees, even if only spruce and fir – hardwoods do not pay in the glens – were calculated to be from £6 to £13 an acre, averaged over seventy years, depending on the quality of the timber, and this profit would come to the landlord alone and not be shared by the tenants. Balanced on the one hand was the length of time it takes to see a return

Looking across at the Allargue Arms Hotel and the home farm at lambing time

from trees – there would now be no half yearly rent – but balanced on the other was the generosity of the planting grant, the fact that there was now no need to improve or maintain steadings, the notional increased capital value of the estate and remission from death duties at the time of death.

J.G. Lockhart pointed out in a passage quoted earlier how changes in public policy can adversely affect upland areas and this remains as true today as in the nineteenth century. 'What is wrong with this country is extreme changes of policies, instead of efficient middle-of-the-road progress', said an official in the Department of Trade and Industry, 'governments swing from one extreme to the other, not only between changes of government but within the lifetime of a single minister'. Frustrated by having no outlet for their objections, feelings in the strath ran high. The Allargue laird, whose father had once owned and sold the land affected, took no part in the arguments, but he felt deeply for the glen and the strath on which his family had spent time, thought and money building up good community relations. 'The trouble in these remote upland areas,' he once said to me, 'is that the people would not buy their own farms even if they were offered to them at a reduced price.' I decided to put the matter to the test. 'Would you buy this farm if you could?' I asked Robbie's wife, who was always cheerful, and whose husband had the quarry for extra income. 'He'd need to bide here himsel',' she replied with a vehemence which surprised me. In Corgarff the thought of retirement to a comfortable little town further down the country is the light at the end of the tunnel keeping the women going through the darkest winter storms.

What was to be done to calm matters down? The laird's reaction was twin track. First, he poured oil upon troubled waters. I did my best to do the same, researching into the matter and attending a difficult meeting where I pointed out that the problem was the blanket generosity of the grant which encouraged the planting of trees on agricultural land. Second, he sold parcels of his heather hill to the Forestry Commission, endorsing the government's need for more trees and trying to keep the balance in the strath between hill and alluvial river planting. Unfortunately, however, for whatever reason, the siting of some of the woodlands was not ideal, and trees are unhappy bedfellows with grouse. As they grew they acted as harbingers for winged and four footed predators, which preyed upon his grouse and interfered with two of his best drives. What he could never have foreseen was that the Forestry Commission, which as a government department he trusted with all the faith of his generation, would in its turn sell off these trees and the land on which they stood to whoever could pay the market value, giving his heirs no alternative but to buy back at considerable cost the forestry and hill that he had formerly judged the estate had not the capital to plant. These matters showed beyond doubt that not only is it very difficult in a strath to achieve the right balance between agriculture, forestry, fishing and game preserve (or what was before the protection of the predator a game preserve), but it is difficult also to choose the right species and position for the actual siting of the trees.

No sooner had the repercussions over these planting policies subsided and the 1968 legislation been restored, so that the tenant had once more the right to hand on a farm tenancy to his son – one family in Corgarff were reputed to have been tenants for 700 years – than another problem erupted over the fishing. There were some salmon in the river further down the strath, but in Corgarff only an occasional salmon swam or jumped up the privately installed hydro ladder into the higher stretches. Instead visitors came every year to the hotel to fish for brown trout, which in preceding centuries could vary in weight from three quarters to five pounds – a photograph taken in 1919 shows twenty half pound trout caught in one day. It was a dry fly river, wet fly rarely tempted the trout to leave the bottom of the pools. A suggestion for the improvement of the salmon fishing came from a government department which wrote to all the riparian owners, suggesting that their officials electrocuted and took out of the river a number of the trout 'tiddlers' which were taking food from the salmon parr. Since they were gentlemen in whose judgement the lairds had trust it was decided to try the experiment which might add to the economy of the area. Unfortunately it had little or no effect on the salmon, but a devastating effect upon the trout. First the less skilful fishermen began to catch fewer reasonably sized trout, and then the experts were affected. What had been an excellent trout river increasingly attracted fewer if any summer visitors. The river now required restocking, but no government department offered to put back the trout that they had taken out and the lairds could not afford to do so. In some people's judgement the advent of acid rain falling from increased afforestation contributed in part to the problem of falling fish stocks.

Unfortunately all this activity took place just as I had time to give up the occasional afternoon's clear water worm fishing, in which the laird's mother had been an expert and which had been a favourite sport in the seventeenth century, in order to try to learn to fish with a dry fly. In clear water worm fishing the line needs no weights, the worm should travel fast downstream with the current of the water and then be cast back upstream into those places where experience tells you to expect the trout to hide. The line should always be taut and concentration must not flag. A little tug should be resisted by what might be called a mini strike. The trout lie beside the eddies and hide behind the stones with their heads upstream, so that it is necessary to wade and stalk them from behind. I found it surprisingly difficult to convert my knowledge of this ancient art, which I had learnt in the war from one of Agnes' visiting friends, into the science of dry fly fishing which requires yet more concentration and skill, but once learnt is devastatingly accurate. I spent time watching the laird fishing in the hope of learning by imitation, but I had chosen just the moment when the number of trout in the river had been substantially reduced. By now even John was finding it difficult to come home with trout in his basket for supper.

As luck would have it friends of Agnes chose this inauspicious moment to present her with a trout smoker as a birthday gift and were invited to dinner to see the new toy in operation. The laird said he could no longer be sure of coming back from the river with large trout. What could be done? Bravely the gardener/handyman stepped into the breach. He went poaching. Using half a salmon parr as bait he extracted a couple of two pounders from the river which normally only relinquishes trout of under a pound in size. Since mine host was also the owner of the river no one else was involved in this illegal act which was not disclosed to the guests. The trout were delicious and, in direct apposition to the reasons for which the small trout had previously been electrocuted and removed from the river, my cousins said to each other that the river would be better off without the two huge trout, since they were undoubtedly cannibals and a menace to the smaller ones. A touch of whimsical illogicality is perhaps a necessary ingredient to make the wheels revolve harmoniously in the remote Highland areas of the kingdom, where the two greatest enemies are the weather and public policy in that order and where the population is so small that no government of whatever political persuasion has any need to take heed of the trials and tribulations of its people.

11

The Community

Not long before I left the glen I was driving past a line of houses in Strathdon when I spotted a small boy in a driveway looking longingly after a ball which had just rolled across the road. The intensity of his gaze and stance so impressed me that I stopped and reversed back to see that he was reunited with it before being tempted to cross the road with a vehicle coming. By the time I got there three older children had come to his rescue. In how many other places I thought as I drove on would so many of us have reacted so speedily to the plight of a small boy. How does the glen teach its children that they must be responsive to the needs of others? Being part of a wider family, people in remote places have a feeling of responsibility not only individually – breeding a fierce independence of spirit – but also for those around them – building up a caring community. This is what the clan system tried to teach within its own region. Integrated into that set of natural rules was the teaching of the early church, which developed into the democratic morality of the Reformation, when fines for perceived wrong doing went into boxes for the poor.

For the past fifteen hundred years the Christian church has been central to the life of the community in these glens, but now after two World Wars have ferociously shaken the cradle of Christendom mankind has allowed his faith in spiritual progress to be eroded, while the church has diluted its moral message and watched congregations shrink. The Corgarff Church was built by the laird's great great grandfather just before the middle of the last century at a time when the Scottish Society for the Propagation of Christian Knowledge (started in 1708) encouraged and undertook a programme of church and manse building throughout the Highlands. Prior to that Presbyterianism was administered from Strathdon church, while Roman Catholics attended a small chapel at the junction with the road to the south and the nearest place of Episcopalian worship was another twenty miles away, following the course of the Don. To reach the present Corgarff church one turns into a rough road opposite the school, goes past the wooden village hall and carries on to a coppice of fir trees which provide some shelter from the east winds blowing up the glen. These winds can turn the Christian calendar upside down, for instead of having the harvest thanksgiving in the autumn, a delayed 'hearst' can postpone it until late on in November or December. Indeed one year it was held a week before Christmas, while it was snowing hard and cars had to be pushed back through the gate after the service. The sheaves of corn were black in the field that year and even those chosen for the service were suffering from dark rot, which had to be hidden by the purple 'neeps'. 'We thank the Lord,' intoned the minister, 'for all the seasons, spring, summer, seedtime, autumn and now here's winter again,' and even as he spoke the congregation could see large snow flakes fluttering down outside the long window behind his head.

One year I took sheaves from the home farm down to the thanksgiving service. 'I hope there are nae mice in them,' said Willie, the beadle, as he took them from me. At the time I thought this was a butt for his humour but later was told that mice rank enemy number one in the Corgarff Church, the devil coming a poor second. Recently it has been reported that they have eaten the inside of the organ and even nibbled away at the black ebony keys. They are, however, not the only rodents responsible for dirt and destruction in the church. Nearly a century ago the laird's wife complained about mouse droppings in her pew and received the cryptic reply, 'Them's nae mice, them's batties.' At that time the minister ruled the congregation with the proverbial rod of iron, the records of the church showing that in the last century any moral and sexual licence was 'preached' from the pulpit as vehemently as in the days of Robbie Burns. Wrongdoers had to be penitent and to make amends. Not all those who attended church were sincere Christians, but nevertheless they had as their ideal Christian values, which they saw as a means of holding the community and individual families together.

The beadle Willie was the elder brother of Doddie, who had come to help us build our road, bringing his plough and his pandrops. One year at the Ball, then held immediately after the Annual Gathering, Willie sat down at one end of our table before Agnes had taken her seat. He was a little fu' and very expansive. 'I'm nae a Christian mind,' he said to me confidentially, 'but the minister had naebody to do the job and I didna like to see him stuck.' His brother's kindness to us was born of the same philosophy. 'When Mrs Stewart comes for help,' he explained to the other guests, 'she aye takes my brither.' This was hardly surprising since, being the eldest of the family, he directed the business of the farm. Then, as if trying to convince himself that the rumours he had heard about me leaving Auchmore were not true, and, with an expansive wave of the hand towards me, he continued, 'She's yin of us noo, she canna leave us noo.' At this point Agnes returned to reclaim her seat and he rose courteously to his feet and bade us au revoir.

Willie had highlighted a truth governing good community values. You do not need to be a committed Christian to further the life of the church or the community, provided you practice Christian values and are a good neighbour. In the glen this spirit has been engendered by centuries of unbroken trust. Someone has always been there to keep the silken thread unbroken. If the church breaks trust then the laird must be firm in his integrity. If the laird breaks trust then the church must stand for abiding values. The church and the lairds, not working together but along parallel lines, have been the two leaders of Highland communities throughout history, with the dominie the uncommitted referee, dependent in the old days on the laird for his salary and on the church for his job, but relying on his learning and sense of history to provide the independence and freedom of thought with which to deliver an unbiased judgement.

In the north of Scotland the influence of individual men and women, such as Duncan Forbes of Culloden, has been far reaching, for there has not been to the same extent a peaceful tradition of Christian thought, teaching and church architecture as existed for much of the time in England. Religious and political wars, both external and internal, criss-cross the pages of Scottish history with such rapidity that great movements forward were followed by years of violence and decline until resurgent inspiration surfaced once again. Nevertheless the origins of Christianity in the north east are both spiritual and romantic, for the area was richly endowed with saints, who arrived on the sea coasts and travelled up the rivers bringing the Christian message. While St Columba crossed the Irish Sea to the west coast, where he founded a mission in Iona, moving northwards via Dunkeld, others like St Ninian came up from Whithorn in Wigtownshire. St Ninian was a Romanised Briton, who, after the Romans had withdrawn and the Angles had invaded Northumbria, pushed up in large numbers into the Lothians, overflowing west and north into areas like Strathclyde. One of St Columba's followers, St Moluch or Moluag, came from Northern Ireland and founded in 566 Mortlach Church in Banffshire, not more than thirty miles over the mountains from Corgarff, which became a bishopric for a hundred years in the eleventh and twelfth centuries. St Machar (or

Mochrieha) could have travelled from there to Corgarff to found his chapel site beside a well of his name, but it is more likely that, as he preached in the neighbouring valleys, he landed on the east coast, following the valleys and rivers for shelter and fish.

Authenticating these stories there are all over the north east of Scotland relics and stones both Pictish and Christian, the latter of which are identified with numerous saints such as Ternan, Fergus, Kentigern, Ffinian, Ethernan, Briach, Nathalan and Drostan, whose arrival is recorded in the Book of Deer. By the time the Scots, Picts and Angles had united in 843 under their first King, Kenneth McAlpine, the Columban Church had absorbed all lesser foundations and accepted the Canterbury date of Easter at the Synod of Whitby in 664. In the Columban Church the abbots were good scholars and, being able to marry, were part of the community, but they had no central organisation or system of land holding, so that the Roman Catholic Church, crossing the Channel under the apostasy of St Augustine, had, by the reign of Malcolm Canmore and Queen Margaret, absorbed the Columban Church, on account of its powerful system of land holding and greater financial strength. David I in the twelfth century consolidated this position, building monasteries in the north east, increasing the number of dioceses, dividing the country into shires and founding a parochial system based on the estate boundaries of landowners, which encouraged the Normans to travel north and become lords of the manor, building churches and appointing clergymen.

In the upland and landward areas such as Corgarff there would have been small chapels, which could also have been used as schools. Because the parish priests had glebes and farmed themselves they were well integrated into the life of the rural communities, but the standard of their learning was not high, borne out by the Pope later sending mendicant friars to poorer areas. All parishes were part of the spiritual and feudal hierarchy, for which the bishops paid homage to the king, holding their land in frank almoign, which imposed the obligation of helping to build royal palaces. Although there is little doubt that in early times the monasteries were rich in music, painting and stone carving and many had schools attached, the bishops owed their appointments progressively to the king and to the rapacious nobility, both of whom appointed relations and bastard sons to vacant sees, men who kept mistresses and were often not consecrated, which brought the church into disrepute. Indeed so concerned was the Pope about the state of the Scottish church that just before the Reformation he gave a grant to take the Lords of Session out of Parliament and into a

College of Justice, so that Parliament could concentrate more on supplying finance to the king, rendering him less dependent on the coffers of the church.

The parish of Corgarff lies just within the Highland line – Gaelic was spoken to within forty miles of Aberdeen – and when the Reformation came it swept up the rivers like a spate, gathering souls into its swirling waters, halting only at the mountain barriers beyond which lay individual clachans and villages still committed to Rome. Because of the lamentable state of corruption into which the church had drifted it is hardly surprising that the reforming movement was supported by lairds as well as people. Not only did it save the Scots from paying teinds, which had found their way into the wrong pockets, but its straightforward moral teaching was in keeping with their fierce spiritual independence and belief in God as the final arbitrator. The General Assembly of 1560 was recognised as the power for redressing church disorders, while the synods, presbyteries and kirk sessions were to be responsible for imposing higher standards of morality. Elders were to be disciplined along with their congregations, fines were to be imposed for non-attendance at church on those who could pay, all church members must have a psalm book and a bible. Differences of belief, however, between high and low church continued to tear the country apart in the succeeding century, with only James VI and I prepared to compromise constructively. The battles of the Civil War and those between the Episcopalians and Presbyterians who had signed the Covenant were every bit as bloody as those previously fought between Roman Catholics and Reformers. It was not until the settlement of 1689, confirmed in the Act of Union eighteen years later, that Scotland's religious denomination was guaranteed. There then followed a period of calm and the building of churches and manses, some of which replaced fabrics destroyed by religious strife – just before the 1715 Rebellion an Act was passed to punish offenders who damaged church buildings in a riot – and this programme of building reached its peak in the early nineteenth century.

Only one last internal spiritual battle remained to be fought in Scotland and Corgarff, among a small minority of parishes, allowed the Disruption within the Church of Scotland to pass it by. The Disruption was sparked off in Perthshire in 1837 when the people of Auchterarder refused to accept a new minister chosen by their patron, Lord Kinnoull. Lay patronage had been re-introduced in 1712, but congregations were allowed to dissent from their patron's choice, with the presbyteries the final arbitrators. Peace reigned for 122 years, but in 1834 the General Assembly passed the Veto

Act in defiance of Westminster and gave the right to appoint a minister wholly to the congregation. When the Court of Session and the House of Lords upheld Lord Kinnoull's right of choice and the Presbytery's final assent, this decision, despite efforts to compromise, lit a spiritual fire which burned for nearly a century, fanned by the eloquence and inspiration of Dr Thomas Chalmers, mentor of the Disruption and founder of the Free Church of Scotland. All over the country ministers preached once more in the open air and within months second churches and manses sprang up in almost every town and village. The glen was spared this disunity, although Strathdon temporarily divided, as did so many other parishes elsewhere. Instead, in 1834, the year of the Veto Act, the chapel by the graveyard was replaced by a new Corgarff church and manse.

Not long afterwards the laird of Newe also built and gifted to the glen the village hall, which stands at the entrance to the church road and has been for more than a century a focus for the social gatherings of the village. Shortly after we moved into the cottage the land on which it stood was sold for the second time as part of the sporting estate which surrounded it. The new laird, Lord Cowdray, asked the people to provide concrete posts for new fencing and to pay rent for the parking place on which stood the war memorial. Each demand was met with the same polite answer, 'That was a gift to the hall by the old laird'. Soon the new laird came to admire the integrity and capacity for hard work of his tenants and once he knew that they were not intending to make extravagant demands upon him he generously laid a new gravel car park and provided electric light for the hall, which remains a venue for dances, entertainments and voluntary societies and also provides a gym and play area for the school.

The summer before we left the glen Sir John Forbes had a plaque built into the cairn on the summit of the Lonach Hill to mark his fifty years as Patron of the Lonach Highland and Friendly Society. The clansmen and the pipe band marched to the top of the hill in full Highland dress and a commemoration was held with speeches of tribute. In the evening there was a celebratory dance in the Corgarff Hall. My cousins did not attend, but they asked Hugh and myself to dinner with the son of a local landowner and sent us all to the dance. While we sat round waiting for the band to strike up we were told that the clansmen were drinking in the hotel. 'The policeman's gone to Aberdeen,' I said hopefully. 'The policeman's nae in Aberdeen,' said his voice beside me, 'he's here.' At this point, Ike, the carrier and Charlie Gordon's brother, came across to the three of us and said, 'I've half a bottle of whisky in my car, will you come and join me.'

With the dance still showing no signs of starting, we trooped out and piled into a small Volkswagen, my son and I in the back, Ike and the Englishman in the front. The bottle did the rounds while we discussed the fishing. Then the back door opened and the policeman's voice said, 'Hae ye room for one more?' continuing after a moment, 'Who has the keys of the car?' All was well. One of the wives had sensibly taken charge of them. Soon the conversation turned to anecdotes and stories from the past. By the time we returned to the dance the cheerful 'burling' of the reels had begun.

Colonel Sir John Forbes presenting commemorative awards at the Lonach Gathering to visiting Atholl Highlanders, with the Duke of Atholl and Mr Gibson McIntosh looking on

Active voluntary societies, which meet in the hall, are a feature of life in the glen. At the end of the nineteenth century, the men of the village formed a Debating Society for the Purposes of Mutual Improvement which was initiated by the minister in 1886. Twelve young men of the village debated once a fortnight on matters of national and local interest. The rules were strict. Every member brought one penny to each meeting, if speakers were more than ten minutes late they were fined three pence, if they had to be called to order more than three times at one meeting they were fined a shilling, if they were absent more than four times their names were struck off the roll. A library was started for the purpose of research into the subjects to be debated, the standard of which was intellectually demanding, reflecting the level of education at the time. 'Was the execution of Queen Mary justifiable?' (Decision No). 'Whether the tradesman or the farmer is the best occupation.' (Farmer). 'Are the clergy more rightly the guardians of education than any other?' (No). 'Is it the love of strong drink or money that has done most for the ruin of the country?' (Money). 'Ought the House of Lords to be ended or mended?' (Mended). 'Should a term of military service be compulsory?' (Yes). 'From what do we derive the most pleasure, hope or memory?' (Hope). 'Was Nelson or Napoleon the greater leader?' (Nelson). 'Which is the most happy, the single or the married state?' (Married). 'Does law or education do the most to prevent crime?' (Education). If the decision hung on a single vote the debate was held again and in the case of the question, 'Is poverty or luxury the most productive of crime,' the decision went one way and then the other. This was a period of great hope in western civilisation and there was trust in the power of learning for its own sake and in political institutions and moral values. 'The lights are going out all over Europe,' said Sir Edward Grey, the Foreign Secretary, at the start of the First World War, 'they will not be lit again in my life time.' They have never burnt again with the same degree of hope, trust, innocence and enthusiasm as were commonplace in the closing years of the last century, with their faith in perpetual progress. By the end of the First World War the Debating Society had become a Rifle Club and so it remained until the start of the Second World War, after which neither club was revived, although there is still a rifle range in Strathdon. Shooting straight had become in the violent twentieth century more necessary for survival than debate.

The other great meeting place in Corgarff is the hotel. This is where news is disseminated and parcels and greetings exchanged. After we left the dance at 1 a.m. on that night of celebration we called in at the hotel because the Englishman was curious to see whether people were still up and about. We were given a warm welcome and offered a drink. The hotel represents another facet of life in the glen. It welcomes outsiders from far off places and provides the link between those who live on the main road and those who occupy outlying farms and cottages. Whether in the car park, the bar or the kitchen the people of the glen converse happily with each other in their own idiom punctuated by long companionable silences. 'Well, well fairmer,' goes a typical conversation. 'Well, well gairdener.' 'Fine weather for the sheep.' 'Grand growing weather for the gairden.' The opening habitual greeting is simply, 'Fine day,' and to the question, 'Phoo are ye',' there are only two answers, 'Fine,' or 'Nae bad.' The former may mean anything from rude to indifferent health, while the latter covers everything from a poor lambing season to imminent death. These are not people who grumble or panic or bore people with their problems. Being stoics they expect life to be hard. Further down the country there is a third answer, 'I'm daein awa'.' That means usually that the person is only just surviving, not doing well at all. This reply is not used in the glen. People either survive or they don't. They are slow to ask for help but ready to offer it, as they do a sweetie or a cup of tea. 'Where did the lamb come from?' Bob's small son asks his mother. 'God brought it,' is her reply. 'Why did God not come in for a cup of tea?' her son logically replies. The kitchen of the hotel is always full of cups of tea – postie has his mid day meal there, surrounded in the spring by lambs thawing out on the stove. The door through from the kitchen to the bar and the scullery is often open and news and humour flow between. In the war, when the Forbes family was living in the hotel the bar was the kitchen, the kitchen was the living room, with a tiny office off it, and the piano, on which Agnes accompanied Nanny and the children as they sang Scottish songs, was in the dining room.

After the war the Allargue Arms Hotel became the great meeting place for the Corgarff members of the Lonach Highland and Friendly Society, as the Colquhonnie Hotel and Lonach Hall are for the clansmen of Strathdon. A great sense of style is natural to the area and permeates the annual Gathering and Games held in August by the Lonach Society, in which the clansmen are at one with their environment, history, traditional garb and qualities of character. On the day of the Gathering the men of Corgarff join the clansmen of Strathdon in an early morning start to their march, stopping at the household of one patron of the games and then another, receiving speeches and hospitality at each halt. They are attired in full Highland dress with cross belts and plaids and carry pikes and battle axes. Twice in the afternoon, led by three halbadiers carrying Lochaber axes, their pipe band and their patron, they twice circumvent the games field, attending a luncheon at the Lonach Hall before the two appearances. Behind the long line of marchers comes a horse and cart for the older and incapacitated members. It is seldom put to use but it always draws good humoured banter from the crowd if there is an occupant. Their colours fluttering in the wind and their pipe majors throwing their maces with confidence and dexterity, watching visitors and local people alike feel a stirring of the blood and a catch at the heart strings. The scene is a step back through the years of history which never fails to delight the watching crowd. Not very long ago the Ball was held on the same evening as the Games, so that, like the fictional Brigadoon, the glens and strath came to life for one day only, but, since the date of the Gathering was moved to Saturday, the formal Ball is held on the following Friday, with only an informal dance on the same evening. Few places have such a strong sense of community as this strath, for it is a truly local event, staged by its own people in a rural and domestic background, with woods, farms, fields, houses and steadings dotting the banks of the rivers and burns.

This sense of being an agricultural community was highlighted in the description of the area in the Statistical Account of 1843. The people, said the Account, are a race of independent farmers, who show patient endurance under privation; they are all literate and have great natural acuteness and sagacity in the management of their own affairs; being grateful for other people's kindness and attention, they retain also a sense of injury; they raise money speedily for charity and relieve distress in their own neighbourhood and abroad, engaging in active benevolence to ease the suffering of their neighbours. These last characteristics are given prominence in the objectives of the Lonach Society, the idea for which was first mooted in 1822 at a bonfire on the Lonach hill to celebrate the coming of age of Charles Forbes' eldest son John, who died at the age of 22. The following year Sir Charles Forbes became the first baronet of Newe and to mark the occasion two plaques – one in Gaelic and one in English – were built into a specially constructed cairn on the Lonach Hill. Also in 1823 the Lonach Highland and Friendly Society came into formal being, its aims being to further among other things the preservation of Highland dress, the support of loyal, peaceable and manly conduct, the promotion of social friendly feelings locally and the setting up of a voluntary fund for members' families. In 1841 the Society decided to host Games as well as its annual march and banquet and these became an annual event, attracting enthusiastic support, both local and from further afield.

Some claim that these Games date back to the days of Malcolm Canmore, but this is not strictly true for early gatherings were primarily a preparation for war, whereas now they are a celebration of community spirit and camaraderie. Meeting in those early days on a mound where now stands Braemar Castle, King Malcolm is said to have organised races for young men on the Braes of Mar to test out potential postal runners, on whose speed and endurance depended the raising of the clans for war by means of the fiery cross, two sticks tied together with the horizontal bar burnt at one end and the other dipped in blood. Although some gatherings may have been for an emergency council or to celebrate a peaceful event, such as the leading home of the 'hearst', the majority were preparations for immediate war to redress a wrong perpetrated against the members of the clan. On these occasions the chief, who held the land on their behalf and whose patriarchal and territorial power was based on kinship with the clansmen, encouraged his school of pipers to celebrate recent heroic deeds with newly composed airs and laments.

Since the Highland line passes through the centre of Strathdon, its people dwell in a buffer zone, drawing their values and strength from both Lowland and Highland traditions. They could not help therefore to have been affected by the 1715 Rebellion, for the Earl of Mar held a hunting party at Kildrummy just prior to the Rebellion, Corgarff Castle was used as a collecting point and the standard was raised in the Braes of Mar. After the Rebellion life in the glens began to change. Some young men emigrated, taking with them a yearning for the country they had left, which brought into being in North America the first Highland Charitable Societies, the aims of which were to buy out the Jacobite prisoners from their indentures, relieve poverty, encourage friendly relations among members, mitigate home sickness and foster a love of Scotland. Then came the 1745 Rebellion with the Young Pretender landing from France and raising his standard in the west. Again some local hide-outs were used to store ammunition and the Prince was joined by Jacobites from the north and east, such as Forbes of Glenbuchat. Britain was at war with France, the year before had been threatened by invasion, and she had suffered defeat at Fontenoy a few months previously. Now she saw a Jacobite army within 120 miles of London, threatening the British government and the Protestant succession. Fear blinds the eye to justice and prompted the draconian measures of the 1746 Proscription Act, banning the wearing of Highland dress, the gathering of clans, the playing of pipes and the carrying of arms. The people of Strathdon and the glens must have been grievously affected by these measures which struck at their way of life. They were probably less affected by the ending of the heritable jurisdictions which altered the system of land holding, for on the whole relations with landlords in the area were good. There were no evictions after 1747 and where there joint farms they were converted into manageable family units. The people of Aberdeenshire, who emigrated to Canada, where the first St Andrews Society started in 1798, were small farmers and farm servants, escaping from the hardness of the soil, the short growing season and the insecurity of tenure.

In the north and west, however, the position was different and Dr Johnson drew attention to this in 1773. 'The clans retain little now of their original character,' he wrote, 'Of what they had before... there remains only their language and their poverty.' Help, however, was at hand, for the Highlanders' plight was generating sympathy in Britain and all over the world. A Highland Society was started in London in 1778 to lobby for the lifting of the Disarming Act and the restoration of Highland dress, and another Society was inaugurated in Edinburgh in 1780. Two years later, towards the end of the American War of Independence, in which France was again a leading protagonist, the British government felt sufficiently secure to repeal the hated Proscription Act. The newly raised Highland Regiments won such a reputation for loyalty and courage during the war – six Highland Regiments were raised, four of which were disbanded afterwards and two retained – and so many Loyalists, who went north from America to settle in Canada, were Highlanders that the Duke of Montrose had little difficulty in steering this legislation through Parliament. Now the dancing of shean trews – a lament for the banning of the kilt – represented nothing more than a painful memory. In 1788 the Northern Meeting was inaugurated, promoting Balls and Games.

Unfortunately changes in the system of land holding took longer to be corrected and Sir Walter Scott spoke and wrote repeatedly against the depopulation of the glens. Ever since he witnessed the trial of Robin Oig (recounted in *The Two Drovers*) for the murder of his English friend – who fought with his fists, while the Highlander fought with his dirk – he wanted to heal the divisions between the English and Lowlanders on the one hand and Highlanders on the other. He wanted to show in a favourable light the 'mores' of the clansmen, to demonstrate their peaceful as well as military virtues. In 1810, during the Napoleonic Wars, in which the Highland Regiments again fought valiantly, he presented to the public his poem *The Lady of the Lake,* about which the country was soon to ring with praise. Scott wove into an intricate plot all the facets of Highland and Scottish life – the codes of courage, honour, courtesy and hospitality, the raising of the clansmen by runners through mountain passes, the magnificent scenery, the friendly influence of a peaceful gathering and games held in the courtyard before the king's castle and the forgiveness of former enemies which flowed from the spirit of the games. Friends tried to persuade him not to risk his fortune upon so controversial a subject, but the poem's success was immediate. It brought men and women from all over the world to see the Highlands and to attend the popular gatherings and games. 'Crowds set off to view the scenery until then comparatively unknown and every house and inn was crammed with a constant succession of visitors'. The message of tolerance and forgiveness in the poem could not have been more manifest, nor the presentation of dramatic scenery combined with courteous hospitality more irresistible.

In 1816 the Braemar Wrights Society was started by the skilled tradesmen of Braemar, becoming the Braemar Highland Society ten years later, while on the other side of the Atlantic, where enthusiasm was just as marked, the Glengarry Highland Society held its first Games in Ontario. Meanwhile in 1822 Sir Walter Scott greeted George IV in Edinburgh, the King attired in full Highland dress. In 1823 the Lonach Society was started in Strathdon, commemorated by an annual march and banquet, the Games following eighteen years later. In 1848 Queen Victoria attended the Braemar Gathering, which became the Braemar Royal Highland Society a year later, with clansmen from Atholl and Lonach attending. In the Highlands and all over Scotland and wherever Scots were in the world, games with traditional sports were held, with hill races, putting the stone, tossing the caber, throwing the hammer, dancing reels and strathspeys, judging the best piping and the best dressed Highlander. While the military skills of the clansmen were channelled into the raising of the Highland Regiments the benevolent skills necessary for peace found their natural expression in annual gatherings, games and balls and in the aims of the Friendly Societies, which helped those in need in the locality and became a philanthropic feature of Scottish life here and overseas. Horizons always beckon and for the first time in their history the Lonach Highlanders did an overseas tour in 1996. Queen Margaret, wife of Malcolm Canmore, was half Hungarian, and to celebrate the eleven hundredth anniversary of the founding of the state, the Lonach Highlanders were invited to do a tour of Hungary, where, in full Highland dress, supported by pipers and drummers and led by their present patron, Major Sir Hamish Forbes, they provided a unique spectacle, drawing very large crowds in the squares of Budapest and in towns and villages across Hungary. The clansmen displayed a 'freshness, openness and vigour which evoked a warm response from the Hungarian people'. At home, the Lonach Gathering is not only an annual commemoration and spectacle. It is also a meeting place for friends from all over the world, since gatherings such as these express eloquently the phrase of the old song, 'We're nae awa tae bide awa. We're nae awa' to leave ye' and the words of the traditional Highland farewell, 'Take care of yourself. Good people are scarce'.

Clansmen marching at the Lonach Gathering

Epilogue

The Worst Storm of the Winter

There are certain days in everyone's life which stand out in the memory from the flat humdrum of ordinary existence. Some are 'golden' days, others are fraught with anxiety and turmoil. One such was the great spring snow storm of 1970 in north east Scotland, which extended almost into May and reinforced my decision to purchase a property nearer to civilisation. The uniqueness of this storm occurring so late in the year and carrying on past the end of the lambing season urged me to set down my experiences of life in this glen in the eastern foothills of the Cairngorms before the recollections were blurred by time passing. The first day of the storm began normally enough in pleasant spring sunshine. Hugh was in his second last year at school and was catching the night sleeper to London and the boat train to the continent, whither he was going to improve his languages. We had inspected one property in the morning and were on our way to another in the afternoon when we ran into a sudden heavy snow storm. Knowing that our two ponies were arriving that day from Perthshire, where they had been wintering, my concern for their welfare made me turn around, cancel the appointment, leave my son at the station and set off on the journey home.

I had gone less than half the distance when I ran into real trouble. Whipped by the savage wind the snow was driving in myriads of flakes against the windscreen. The wipers, like two tired arms, struggled back and forth, pushing the snow to one side and then the other. Fog and blizzard reduced visibility to fifteen yards and the car, steamed up with heat, gave a false impression of security. If conditions were like this on the low ground what would it be like in the hills? Although 31 March was late in the year for a real blizzard, caution and experience made me stop at an hotel and telephone for a report from home.

'Oh, it's a wild night here,' said Lottie, the postmistress. The north east Scot has a never-failing capacity for under-statement, and their warnings should be heeded.

'Has the float arrived with the ponies?' I asked, and receiving a negative answer hazarded the question, 'Will it come tonight?'

'Oh surely no.' The tone of her voice conveyed anxiety, and I inquired further.

'Will I get home?'

'Oh well, I dinna ken.' The people of the glen prefer not to commit themselves or to speculate upon uncertainties.

'A float went down the road not half an hour ago.'

This was an accurate picture of the facts. It was lucky, however, that I decided to be warned by her hesitation and to telephone first to the local carrier for news of the ponies, for that float stuck on a bad corner half a mile down the road and had to wait for the snow plough.

'There's no word of the ponies,' said the carrier's brother. So similar were their voices that I thought it was 'himself', 'but you'll have to find a shed here when they arrive. We'll need the float in the morn.'

My heart sank. There was no way that I could visit farms on a night like this. I decided to try and arrange the ponies' future by telephone and if necessary to take a room for the night at the hotel. Increasingly desperate inquiries brought – unusually – no offer of hospitality.

'Oh no, I'm sorry,' said the farmers' wives, 'every shed is full of beasts, hay or straw.'

Mine host came through from the bar in his shirt sleeves, 'Excuse me interrupting, but I overheard your conversation. Your horses would be welcome here for the night. I can put them up with mine'.

Almost before I had time to thank him the telephone rang again. This time it was Charlie, the carrier, and he was the bearer of better news.

'That was my brother you spoke to. I've just come in. Aye, our voices are the same, but he's maybe a wee bit deeper with his humour. I've got a place for your ponies.' By now this seemed a miracle. 'They can find everything they want, stable, hay, water, at Bouties.' This was the Boultenstone Hotel on the way over from Deeside, where his sister, Elma McBain, was 'minding the licence' for the evening, while her daughter and husband went to a wedding.

'As soon as I have word of where they are I'll let you know.'

Hours later his voice came over the wires again. The driver had telephoned from a cottage at the foot of a steep hill blocked with snow. A tanker and tip-up lorry were in collision, the tip-up lorry was on its side and the tanker slewed across the road, with the police and oil company arguing about moving them. Everyone was waiting for the plough and the break down lorry.

I went to bed listening to the sound of wind muffled with snow and imagining that, with spring on its way, the morning would bring better things. Certainly it brought the sun and at first a blue sky, but quantities of snow had fallen in the night more typical of a January storm. A man was shovelling snow from the doorstep of his shop.

'I've never seen anything like it in my life,' he said, 'nae at this time of year. It's more snow than we had a' winter and there's plenty more where it came from.'

At the back door of the hotel were two Hydro Electric landrovers covered with snow. In the kitchen the men were breakfasting, having failed to make their objective the night before even in these sturdy machines. As they dressed in gumboots, white stockings, oilskins and souwesters I stepped into my car and set out on the twenty mile journey to the carrier and twenty-eight mile journey home.

The road was bumpy and rutted with snow and in places the wind was blowing the drifts back over the white surface. The blue sky did not give me its assurance for long and soon renewed blizzard and flakes of snow brought visibility down to a few yards. Between showers the beauty of the scene was breathtaking. Trees, laden with snow on the windward side, drooped over the road with the imagery of fairyland. When woods gave way to open country the mountains continued the upward roll of the white fields without interruption, smooth as the icing on a Christmas cake, with only the merest peep of fence or dyke appearing through the snow.

A cup of coffee welcomed me at the carrier's office, where Charlie was waiting for calls concerning his next day's orders. So far he only had one lorry and driver on the road out of a team of six; the others were all stranded somewhere.

'Your ponies, the float and the driver are all stuck at Bouties, where they arrived at midnight and they are comfortable and welcome. The plough has not been along that road this morning. I think I'll be off to a hot climate instead of biding in one where it snows for seven months of the year.'

I asked if the plough had been up the road towards Corgarff.

'Nae yet, but it's bound to be on its way in a wee while.'

I settled down in the cosy room to enjoy the coffee made by the carrier's niece who had been stranded at her mother's house, while her mother had been stranded at theirs. Her grandparents had run their carriers' business from this address and their kindness and hospitality to all and sundry had become a legend throughout the area. She assured me they were delighted to have the horses as guests, but recounted how the night had brought disaster in other ways. The local doctor had suffered his third coronary heart attack. Waking at 2 a.m. and, not wanting to disturb his wife, he had waited till 4 before rousing her, by which time, in her words, he was 'like wax'. His son alerted the local snow plough, which set out on the twenty mile journey to fetch the nearest doctor who, in his landrover, was intermittently having to stop and dig his way up the road through drifts. Once this was accomplished it then took three hours for the ambulance to reach the nearest hospital, forty seven miles away, but despite the delay the doctor was holding his own. The story threw a blanket of concern over the room interrupting the usual humour brought by bad weather.

'What are you going to do now?' Charlie asked.

I decided to ring John's sister, Kitty, to see if I could stay at Newe with her and her sister Betty until the road was opened further up the glen, but, as the number rang out, a driver came in to say that the plough was starting up the road. Hearing this report and undeterred by the weather, Kitty said that she intended going to Allargue in her landrover for lunch and would be pleased to give me a lift or a lead. I decided, perhaps foolishly, to take my car but thought it would have been wise on such a day for us to follow the plough immediately. Unfortunately, however, Kitty had lost a dog among the plantation of fir trees. This delayed us and by the time we started, it was difficult for my car to keep up with her landrover through the thick snow. I thought too late that it would have been wiser to leave it in the village. When the wind blew the snow across the road visibility became a white impenetrable wall. Soon I could see nothing in the blind drift and as the road went higher the drifts on either side rose to above a man's height. With a blizzard hitting me on one of the worst and most notorious corners, I could not distinguish the road from the wall of snow in the swirling fog of flakes. Knowing, however, every turn and twist, I guessed where the gap should be and came through, astonished at my own good fortune. Now, as the incline increased, the wheels began to spin in the deep snow, but no sooner had I decided to abandon the car than I saw the landrover stopped ahead. Figures huddled in warm coats emerged from the post office to greet me. The red GPO landrover was parked by the door.

'I'll see you up if you follow me,' said Jock Philip, the postie, so I ran my car off the road, transferred everything into Kitty's landrover and went on behind postie into an even thicker blizzard. On the next corner his landrover stopped and re-started. We stopped but did not immediately re-start and so lost sight of our leader. Now we were ploughing about in drifts

Digging out the plough

of snow and the wheels were spinning and skidding, even in four wheel drive. Visibility and progress were nil. I climbed out into the freezing cold and saw that the track we were on led into an eight foot drift, but my directions to the driver were carried away on the wind. With the landrover stalled again I tried unsuccessfully to push it back on to the correct narrow track. I was bitterly cold for, having set out on a clear day with no snow, I had no trousers, only gumboots which I always carried in my car. Suddenly a shape loomed out of the fog. It was postie's landrover reversing towards us. Again I tried to shout but could not be heard above the wind. Then, numb with cold I realised our landrover was in motion and, running alongside, jumped in to avoid a further halt in the deep snow.

At last the final five in one hill rose before us. Postie raced up, stuck and reversed back. We decided not to risk it and transferred parcels to the red landrover. Postie took another run at the hill, stuck, slewed across the road and abandoned the vehicle, having made considerable height. Now we carried everything through the deep snow. My parcels grew heavier.

'Put them in the Father Christmas sack,' said Jock from behind me, hearing my puffs.

'Are you sure it won't make it too heavy for you?' I asked and received the usual reply, 'Not at a'. You're very welcome.'

The blizzard was still swirling about as we tumbled over the threshold of my cousin's house, warm, friendly and brimming with hospitality. A tot of whisky was ready for Jock.

'There's a bed here if you want it,' said Agnes to me with characteristic hospitality after we had eaten lunch. But like a person with 'bends' I was suffering from that extraordinary, but well known, sensation of, 'I must beat it' that comes with snow and felt that I must go down to my own house to check if everything was all right and fetch some suitable clothing – an unnecessary journey. What I did not know then was that standing out in the blizzard with no protective clothing had affected the circulation of my knees, a warning that would perhaps have made it wiser not to venture forth again that day. Extreme cold to parts of the body brings with it the risk of cold blood carried back to the heart.

As I set off the snow was still falling and lying two feet on the flat and much more in drifts. At each laboured step the snow was above my knees, filling my gumboots. The gale was in my back but the air was intensely cold, making it difficult to breathe even on the way down the hill. Drifts of snow surrounded the sitting room window, feet high, but luckily the wind had not blown the snow towards the door of the cottage, otherwise I could not have got in. I changed into thick sweater, trousers and ski boots, collected my night things into a rucksack and started back up the hill, but the snow was so deep that I made little progress. I returned and put on my skis, but the snow was soft as cotton wool so that they sank deep into it, adding to the weight of each step and rendering progress impossible. I carried them back into the cottage and set off again on my feet. More than once on the return journey I thought I would not make it. Very slowly and with ever-increasing pauses, facing downhill away from the wind in order to get my breath before it was whipped away by the gale, the hill was conquered. Yet even when I saw John with his little grandson in the distance and was at last on the flat ground I still had an extraordinary urge to give up and lie down. I knew now a little of that irresistible feeling that years ago had killed a local lass as she struggled homewards in a raging blizzard over the hills behind. I knew also that I was now too old to live in such a precarious situation so far from a proper road.

For two subsequent days there was little movement in the glen. The plough came up in the morning in front of the postal landrover and anyone requiring urgently to leave or arrive travelled behind it. Although the gale had dropped the snow continued to fall, building upon earlier amounts, with huge drifts not only along the dykes and fences but anywhere where the wind had blown it into hummocks. On the third day the ponies arrived by lantern light at ten p.m. and were shut into the stable behind my cousin's house. When I asked their hosts at the hotel, 'What am I owing you?' I received the usual reply, 'You're nae owin' us naethin' – they were our guests.' As the ponies unconcernedly munched the sweet smelling hay, which had fortunately been delivered the day before the blizzard began, they conveyed an impression of faith in the hospitality and efficiency of humankind, as though this was the quality of food to be expected at fourteen hundred feet at the end of one of the severest winters on record.

Had they but known, it was very nearly not so, for, 'Hay is fetching £25 a ton if you can get it,' I'd been told on my arrival home the week before. Fortunately, however, Charlie, the carrier, had a friend who tossed the caber at the Lonach Gathering and who might have a ton to spare.

'But it's all away,' the friend said when I telephoned him.

'Oh, what a pity,' I replied, 'I only wanted a ton.'

'Oh maybe I'll find some over, perhaps I could spare you fifty bales from what's lying around.'

Cautiously, approaching on a curve, I sought further information and the conversation continued in a manner typical of the glen.

'And if you did have fifty bales, what would you charge for them?'

'Oh, maybe £16. It's fetching £18 further south.'

'And if you could manage this how would I get it from you?'

'The carrier will be in aboot next week and if there's room in the lorry he'll take it back for you.'

Two days later the hay arrived, and if it had not been for this kindness and efficiency the ponies would have been starving. Instead they gave an air of placid contentment completely at odds with the wildness of the weather beyond the stable door. During the next weeks of continuing blizzard showers they saw nothing of the outside world except for a walk round the house and a roll in the snow, after which on one occasion, jerking the rope from my hands, the New Forest gelding disappeared over a four foot drop into what looked like level snow and immediately was down and plunging.

By now, however, the snow had begun to settle and the skiing was improving. It had been very fast behind the snowplough, but the machine was currently stuck at the top of the hill with a broken half shaft. Going up to inspect we explored the extraordinary snow ledges and hillocks of snow which we could see from below. The unusually strong north wind had lifted all the snow from behind the unfenced larches on the hilltop and deposited it lower down above the fenced plantation, leaving the upland northern slopes bare. In places the snow looked like wind-swept sand dunes and in others it had formed miniature castles with high precipes ready to avalanche, which were twice the height of a man. Nothing like it had been seen before and we took photographs and informed the media who did not believe us and did not come to see for themselves. The longer the snow lay the better the skiing became and John, Agnes and I were out every day on long runs, but I was puzzled by my painful knees, which I thought was rheumatism. When it turned out that I had phlebitis caused by exposure I was warned off such activity and told to rest. It was lucky no one realised this before because I would have missed some splendid skiing.

Faced with such a prolonged period of storm the birds were daily growing weaker and many were dying. The only patches where food could be found were on the grass showing through the snow in front of the house. Here the running water of an impromptu little stream washed the snow clear as soon as it fell. While the blackbirds, tits, robins, warblers and chaffinches came to the bird table daily to eat the rusks and oatmeal put out for them, the peewits and a single curlew strutted disconsolately up and down the bare patch of grass, reluctant or too tired to fly away even when disturbed by the dogs. Although the lambing season – always late at this height – was not due to start for another day or two, half a dozen lambs were already being born each night. Some were smothered by snow, some took a few steps in the intense cold and died. Those that survived the shock of their birth were shut with their mothers into a snug railway wagon bedded with straw. Each day the tractor, fitted with a snow plough, cleared a fresh route for the flock to travel from their field by the steading, where they were fed with hay, to the turnip field, where the wind had blown patches of snow from off the turnips. Penned into small areas the sheep huddled together for warmth.

Between showers of snow the April sun was bright and the snow-covered mountains and fields were exquisitely beautiful. The river wound its way through the valley like a black snake. Here and there bulges of snow drooped over its banks, in places nearly joining across the water. Birches along the banks, clad in brown winter garments, were surrounded by white marshes, from whose depths peeped the tips of rushes. Black lines of fences rising through the snow divided the valley into squares and enclosed the clustered homesteads, half now unoccupied. Because of the almost uninterrupted whiteness the eye travelled at speed over the eight white mountains ringing the valley, making a wide panorama out of what were usually individual scenes. Then, as one looked, the sun faded as if a shutter had been drawn across a light and flakes of snow, increasing in number and size, swirled again across the valley. Simultaneously the sky changed to the same colour as the snow and a blanket of blizzard was once more wound like a shroud over the glen.

My cousins kindly persuaded me not to go back to my own house until the storms were over, for it was now almost buried by snow. I was grateful for their hospitality because, without each other's companionship, the enforced confinement would have affected morale. Whenever the laird went down the road after the plough to a meeting, a funeral or a roup, he came back with unusually generous provender which made mealtimes a relaxation. As we dined on the eleventh evening of the storm off avocado pears, tinned pheasant and excellent hock, a dying butterfly, which had been in the dining room throughout the siege, alighted on my head, as if in need of help and sustenance. 'Would it like apple peel or a little wine?' I asked, prompted by the improbability of its rash behaviour.

'I wonder if we shall be overtaken by the glaciers on top of the hill like the dinosaurs from previous centuries, who were suddenly frozen in ice where they stood,' observed the laird. 'Perhaps we should all hurry further down the glen before it happens to us too.'

Every night we looked at the sky and every morning hoped that this would be the end of the storm. But always the sky told us the opposite. Each day John was out with his sheep or to be found digging his way along the drive or going up or down the hill to communicate with the snowplough. He was proud of his snow-digging technique and showed the road men how he greased his shovel with Vaseline so that the snow slid from it more readily. Tired out by his work in the evening he slept by the fire or finished the crossw   puzzle or played on a flute which he had cut from the dried stem of a giant hogweed plant. A soldier with a distinguished war record in Norway and India, he had been trained to maintain morale with humour and to balance the evening's dreary conversation about the dying butterfly and the dinosaurs, he now diverted our attention with his wide repertoire of tricks with which in the summer he sometimes amused his guests on wet days.

'Last night,' said the keeper, Geordie Cheyne, disconsolately in the morning, as he kicked the snow from his boots at the door, 'I saw the new

118

moon on its back. I don't know what that means.'

'It's the ballad of Sir Patrick Spens,' I replied.

'I saw the old moon late yestreen, with the new moon in her arms,' the keeper continued. 'And should we go to sea, my lord, Methinks we'll come to harm.'

The things that have kept me in this glen I thought, as I trudged through the snow to water the horses are the intellectual ability of the people, their courage, humour, hospitality, kindness and the warmth of their hearts. How can I leave them? 'They've warm hearts, that's why we come back year after year to fish,' an Englishman had said to me at breakfast, while I was staying in the hotel, stranded by the storm. 'If they had not they'd freeze to death.'

As consumer-led civilisation and centralisation, combined with the rigours of the weather, frog march the people away from the farms and glens, it is important to recall the life of this ancient community, which, surrounded by some of the finest scenery in the world, reverences warmth of heart, hard work and intellectual and courageous endeavour above material or selfish advance. 'In too many instances,' wrote Sir Walter Scott, 'the Highlands have been drained, not of the superfluity of population, but of the whole mass of the inhabitants, dispossessed by an unrelenting avarice, which will one day be seen to be as short-sighted as it was selfish. Meantime the Highlands may become the fairy ground for romance and poetry or the subject of experiment for the professors of speculation, political and economical. But if the hour of need should come and it may not be far distant, the pibroch may sound through the deserted region, but the summons will remain unanswered.' How true! There are now in many places in the Highlands only the deer and the birds of prey to hear the echoes of its call.

Just before we left the cottage and not long after man's first trip to the moon, when the clouds in the sky at the time of sunset had gone rushing past as if awakened and stirred, I had an extraordinary dream. I was at Allargue and the house had become airborne and was a space capsule travelling round the earth. Everyone in the house was performing their usual function, adapted to the extraordinary situation in which they found themselves. John kept going back and forth to the boiler room to check the instruments on the hot water boiler which now told him where we were and how fast we were travelling. A most considerate host he repeatedly left the fireside in the evening, when one was staying in the house, to check on the temperature of the water for his guests' baths. Characteristically, Agnes was standing by the stove in the kitchen, cooking for a large household. She was also cleaning silver cups, which were laid out on the table. Equally characteristically her guests were helping her, while she was saying as she so often did, 'We must keep up the standards'. It seemed in no way odd that the little silver animals were also being cooked in the stew. Meanwhile Mr Webster, the gardener handyman, who had been such a help to me in Auchmore with his support and advice, was going round the house checking to see whether cracks were appearing caused by the pressure of the atmosphere. 'Will the house stand up to the strain?' I asked anxiously. 'Oh yes,' he replied as was his wont, 'It's made of very good material.'

The house, the glen, the strath and the people who inhabit them are made of very good material, constant as the granite with which they are surrounded. In recounting dreams one lays oneself open to disbelief. Yet what the old shepherd said to me on the road is as true of the story of the dream as it is of the whole of the narrative recounted in this book, 'It's nae a story, it's true.'

Miss Betty Forbes on her way to Allargue

Appendix

The following papers concerning the Forbes family and the estate of Newe, Strathdon, were retrieved by refuse men 20 years ago from a dustbin in Aberdeen, to which they had mercifully been consigned by the professional administrators of the estate. 'The evil that men do', said Shakespeare, 'lives after them, the good is oft interred with their bones'. Predominant among the gentlemanly virtues of that time was one which precluded any mention of good works done by a person on behalf of others and therefore twentieth-century history is often slanted through understandable ignorance. Grateful acknowledgement must be made to the anonymous refuse collector whose diligence produced these records. (The words are spelt as in the original text.)

Extracts from the original list of the Names of Tenants and Inhabitants of Skellater, Corgarff and New, who came to Sir Charles Forbes, Bart. at Edinglassie in October and November 1825:

Anderson, Penelope, in Heughhead, occupies a cottage, requests permission to continue tenant. The cottage is out of repair, it requires stones for the house, as well as thatch for the roof, she employs herself in and out doors labour and in spinning shirting, she has a daughter who supports her partly by her labour.

Her request to be granted, when convenient, subject to the tenant of the farm paying him one shilling a year.

Abercrombie, Jannet, widow of Henry Michie, occupies a small farm at £10.13.7.d her husband was lost in the snow, the expenses of his funeral were £7.10.- she gratefully acknowledges Sir Charles generosity to her on that account, she has nine children, offers her blessing to Mr Charles Forbes for his kindness to her, she will consult John McHardy about making an offer for her farm.

Approved, and to be arranged as Mr Stewart and Ordgarff may agree upon.

Brooks, Margaret, at Ordachoy Corgarff, single woman, now lives with widow Farquharson at Luib, she formerly had a room in Corgarff Castle as a school-room, but was turned out by Norman McHardy when Sir Charles Forbes purchased the property, she wants a cottage for a school at Corgarff. John McHardy will give her a character. She never brewed whiskey.

It is apprehended that this woman's character will not bear enquiry.

Campbell, Elizabeth, widow lives in the same cottage with Jannet Downie widow, and both are assisted by the parish, wishes to have a house put up for her and Jannet Downie.

Promised, subject to the tenants and paying one shilling a year.

Downie, Jane, widow of Culnabaichan tenant of the farm, which she transferred to her brother-in-law, Francis Downie, who gave her a dwelling, with keeping for a cow and horse and leading her firing. Wants a lease in her own name, she is lame of her hand and cannot work or manage the farm herself.

An arrangement to be made with Francis Downie, for the widow to be taken care of as heretofore.

Downie, Margaret, widow of John McHardy of Easter Corryhoul rents a farm at £13 a year, she has nine children and wishes to be continued tenant, she has brewed whiskey and has been several times fined.

Agreed.

Durward, Catharine, occupies half of a cottage at Corgarff under her brother-in-law, who has treated her unkindly and has put his horses in the other end of the cottage, and has taken the key of the cottage from her.

Sir Charles desired the Revd. Mr Forbes to speak to her brother on the matter.

Fife, Barbara, in Delavine, widow of John Downie holds a cottage under widow Dunbar, her husband was lost in the snow, no rent has been asked since her loss, has one son at home in bad health, her other son is in Jamaica but she has not heard of him, her daughter married a soldier 92nd Regiment, paid 12/11d for her cottage and 4/11d for a kale yard, wishes to have her cottage and kale yard.

To have her cottage and kale yard subject to the tenant paying one shilling a year.

Glashan, Elizabeth, wife of the tailor opposite New, want his house repaired or a new one built in a better situation, Dr Forbes permits her to cut grass for her cow in the plantation, she pays no rent, has lived twelve years in the cottage.

William Ross in Little Telley to be spoken to in favour of this request.

McPherson, Jane, Lochside, Corgarff, single woman, daughter of John McPherson, she was born in Ireland, her mother was Jane Stewart of Corgarff. Dr Forbes gave her the ground for her house and the Country built it for her. John McHardy is very kind to her, every one speaks well of him, has paid no rents, her house is in bad repair, she has a son by Alexander Fife.

To be allowed to keep possession of her cottage, paying a shilling yearly to the tenant, Sir Charles has spoken to Ordgarff.

McHardy, Anne, widow of James McHardy in Ordachoy, occupies a farm in Corgarff, rent £18. wishes to have a road across the Don to the haugh and will assist in making a bulwark to prevent inundation, she has eight sons, the eldest 21.

To be arranged satisfactorily for the poor woman on straighting marches.

McHardy, James, in Easter Corryhoul, he and his brother hold a farm at Corryhoul and wish to continue tenant, which Sir Charles promises on their offering a fair rent and taking good care of Margaret Downie the mother.

Agreed, straighting marches.

McHardy, Susan, widow had occupied a cottage at Wester Corryhoul, eleven years, at 10/- a year, her husband built it and she wishes to have it rent free. She keeps it in repair, she has two sons, one apprentice to a shoemaker, the other is a servant and gets £3 wages, she never brewed whiskey.

Agreed.

McHardy, Elizabeth, in Shinnach occupies a cottage, she has lived there 18 years and pays £3 a year, she wants her cottage repaired, Sir Charles will let her have wood from Skellater and John Simpson her brother-in-law will assist in repairing her cottage.

Agreed.

Munro, Charles, tailor at Ordachoinachan to have wood for a house afforded him by Sir Charles Forbes, the house to be built on the north side of the burn at Tornahaish, and to have liberty to improve a yard for himself, provided it is so fenced as to give no trouble to his neighbours.

Philip, John, and Jannet Stewart his wife, Mill of Garchory.

Very deserving people, all their requests appear reasonable and to be complied with.

Stewart, John, in Delnadow, lives in a grass house under George Farquarson, he is a carpenter and pays £1 a year, wishes to have a piece of ground near his house for a kale yard and if a tack should become vacant he would wish to take it. Saw the moor on fire in July last, he and Charles Wattie put it out.

Promised on his giving up whiskey brewing.

Stewart, Arthur, in Delachuper, pays £7.10.11. for his farm, it is much flooded by the Don, Sir Charles will allow wood to make the Bulwark and all the tenants must assist in this work, wishes to be a member of the Lonach Club.

Simpson, John, in Shinnach, came by desire of Elizabeth McHardy, acknowledges his kindness to the poor woman and promises to continue it and to assist in repairing the house and byre, he wants wood for repairing his own house, which Sir Charles will order for Skellater.
Granted.

Extracts from the Memorandums:

It is Sir Charles Forbes's orders that all the Corgarff tenants be bound to proper rotations in croping, according to printed regulations.

The wood of Lonach to be reserved for the Corgarff tenants, the sale of which to be taken in charge by William Stewart carpenter.

Moss Greives, whose duty it shall be to allow the tenants to cast only as much peats as may be necessary for their dwelling houses.

The Corgarff houses to be thatched with heather, the size to be in proportion to the size of the farm, attention to be paid to the situation of the buildings.

To have a good peat stack at Edinglassie from the tenants of New.

Sir Charles to grant wood for a bridge at Garchory and an iron chain to secure the same from being carried away by the river. This for the accommodation of the children going to school and to be made safe for that purpose.

Walls of the Mill of Garchory to be raised and repaired – a new roof, and slated, Drying Kiln, on the end, and in a line with the Mill, the front of the Mill to be causewayed and kept clean.

Site of cottages for poor people, proposed on the hillock immediately to the west of the little burn of Garchory.

Sir Charles was pleased to order £5 for assisting in providing a schoolmaster, accommodation to be had for the School at Ord or at Garchory. Also £5 for the use of the School at the Castle of Corgarff, a Room being allowed for that purpose.

Sir Charles has agreed to make the road up Noughty Side to join Lord Fife's property, on a plan to be finished by Mr Shear, it being understood that Lord Fife and Auchernach to continue the road through their property.

It is Sir Charles' desire that I encourage his tenants to neatness and cleaness inside and outside their dwelling houses and neat kale yards and corn yards, premiums to be given to those who excell.

The north bank of Polduillie Pot to be planted as soon as the trustees of the Turnpike Road build a dyke along the top of the brae.

It is Sir Charles' orders that the first thing to be looked at by way of improvement is comfortable dwelling houses to his Corgarff tenants.

The poor people are to have their houses built with mortar and harled with lime.

The office houses of Bellabeg to be thatched with broom as soon as possible.

It is Sir Charles' orders that I send a printed copy to each of his tenants in the Lands of New in order to let them know that he wishes them to drop smuggling entirely.

It is Sir Charles' desire that there may be some variety in the plans of the Corgarff dwelling houses; Mr Robison the architect to be sent for to Elgin.

Extracts from Improvements, Repairs, Works suggested by John Forbes, Esq. MP, in October 1826:

William Duguid to have his house lathed below the joists east end and some other small repairs in order to make him more comfortable and to have a cart load of peats from the stack at Edinglassie.

Plantation of Polduillie to be extended. Some small plantations to be made in the policies behind the House of Edinglassie, the greater part of the plants to be of oak and birch.

Mr Forbes agrees for Sir Charles Forbes Bart, to Mr Ross' request of paying the proportion of expenses affecting the Lands of New, Edinglassie and Skellater, for fitting up the garrets of School House of Tarland supposed to be about £3.

John McHardy in Tornahaish to get as much wood gratis from Lonach as is necessary for a bridge on the Burn of Tornahaish by the side of the Commutation Road. John McHardy drives the wood and erects said bridge at his own expense.

Willows to be planted on each side of the Burn of Whittock, Edinglassie.

Extract from Memorandums by John Forbes, Esq. MP, when at Edinglassie in 1827:

The Revd Mr Forbes, Lainorn, to have the Manse repaired in a temporary manner, such as he may consider necessary for his comfort for a time.

John Forbes, Esq., MP wishes to be reminded to apply to Government for that part of the Government Park lying west of the Castle, as it lies in the way of James McHardy's cattle, in going to their pasture, but does not wish to exclude the troops stationed in the Castle from the privilege of exercising thereon.

A contract is drawn up at Edinglassie on 16 Nov. 1825 under which 'Sir Charles Forbes, Bart. proposes that all his tenants above the Mill of Rippachie, Deskryside, join in making a road from Chapelton to the said Mill, Sir Charles paying one half of the expenses and his tenants the other half'.

Summaries of meetings at Edinglassie 29th–31st October 1828. Present: John Forbes, Esq., Revd G. Middleton and D.D.:

The tenants came forward in turn to discuss their new leases and their financial implications. Prices for the standard nineteen year lease range from £6/10s to £21. In discussions upon commodities, such as stones lying at the Mill of New, for which a yearly rent for £40 was agreed, comparisons were made with prices in 1745, 1753 and 1754. The 1822 Act 'for better preventing private distillation in Scotland' had just been passed in Westminster. Stills which had not been 'guaged and stamped' by officers of the Crown were to be forfeited and the proprietors were to be fined or, if no payment was made, imprisoned. The penalty for obstructing an officer was likewise. Each tenant states his own position in this matter, with particular reference to his part in the attack on an officer and the rescue of Farquharson, a tenant on the estate. William Stewart of Boggach 'denies whiskey brewing, or at least has had very little concern in it since Sir Charles was in the country (from India) further than clearing his hand of old stock. Denies poaching and any concern in the rescue of Farquharson or attack on Mr Yates, acknowledges that he authorised one of his servants to kindle a moor not far from his houses for the sake of getting much-feal, and the burning extended further than intended, say some hundred yards, six or seven years ago he was caught in the act of poaching and says he immediately afterwards sold his gun and has given up poaching'. 'Robert Downie Boilmore does not deny that his family have been concerned in whiskey brewing during the last few years and he admits they have done so by his direction. Adheres to the offer of £7 which he sent in last year. Saw the people going down the country, for the rescue of Farquharson, but being on the opposite side of the river he did not make out who they were, or any of them, as they wanted their coats. Denies all connection with muir burning or that he ever poached and the assault on Yates'. One tenant offering for or a new lease admits to having been imprisoned owing to being unable to pay the fine. Another tenant 'a widow's son appeared, not listened to because of the suspicions attaching to him'. Some tenants 'deny every delict as charged against the other tenants'. Others admit brewing up to two or three years ago. Two subtenants were 'told by Mr Forbes that no subtenants were to be allowed and independently of this, that they were both suspected on good grounds of having been concerned in the rescue of Farquharson, for which reason and because of their character generally it was resolved that they should not remain on the estate and they were desired to take themselves off accordingly'. Peter McHardy, Blacksmith 'wished leave to cultivate part of the moor land near his house which Mr Forbes approved of and said he might depend on every encouragement. A dwelling house and smithy have been built for him by Sir Charles'.

In November there followed a change of factor and a summary of the character and ability requirements for a new factor. In December 1828 there are further meetings, and reports continue until June 1835. In December an offer to pay in kind by a tenant was rejected, with suggestions as to the marketing of the commodities, but the following year a tenant was allowed to deliver 2 bols of English coal in lieu of his agreed share of peats. In 1829 the gardener recommended that of the five or six thousand seedling trees required, one fifth be of larch and the rest Scotch firs. In that year some common land was enclosed by tenants, with abatement to those not benefiting. In December disputes arose between tenants over the grinding of malt, many of which involved the supply of water. Also requests were made to the heritor to carry out draining projects, some of which had been referred to in the Memorandums, and proposals were made for river and burn straightening, and bulwarking with brushwood, to be undertaken by the laird or by the tenants with arrangements for compensation. In June 1830 mention is again made of roadside common land, which in Genernan provided sufficient pasture for 500 sheep. Regarding proposed building projects, both of houses and byres, materials were to be provided by Sir Charles with work done by the tenants, sometimes with valuation at the end of the lease, sometimes not. In June 1831 the present road to Corgarff was opened, built by Sir Charles, 'Visited the new turnpike road and went to its upper end at Cockbridge. The situation of the toll should be at Colnabaichan, immediately eastward of the point at which the Glaschal road by Tornahaish takes off to Deeside. Get sanction of the trustees and learn whether a toll-keeper could be accommodated with any of the Colnabaichan houses, without the expense of building. The bridge over the

Don at Luib as well as the other bridges on the line of the turnpike need to be pinned and harled'. In August 1833 a new road is prospected by the estate from Badnagoach through Rippachie to the Deskry Water to join up with the existing road at Broomhill.

Unfortunately at this point the accounts end. What they have revealed is the remarkable diligence and ability of the tenants, in house and byre building, the straightening and bulwarking of rivers and the construction of roads, and their, almost without exception, kindness to each other. They have also told the story of the generosity and wise jurisdiction of the laird Sir Charles Forbes, Bart., MP, who lived at a time of great philanthropy. The span of his life, 1773–1849, coincided, perhaps not entirely by chance, with that of Stephen Grellet, 1773–1855, to whom the following famous passage has been attributed: 'I expect to pass through this world but once; any good thing therefore that I can do or any kindness that I can show to any fellow-creature let me do it now; let me not defer or neglect it for I shall not pass this way again'.